<u>It's another Quality Book from CGP</u>

Want to hear the <u>bad news</u>? There's a heck of a lot of tricky stuff they expect you to learn for KS3 Spanish.

Want to hear the <u>good news</u>? Good old CGP have got it all covered. We've produced this brilliant book with all the words, phrases and grammar bits clearly laid out and explained.

...d then, in the spirit of going the extra mile, we've put some daft bits in to try and make the whole experience at least vaguely entertaining for you.

We've done all we can — the rest is up to you.

D1581264

<u>What CGP is all about</u>

Our sole aim here at CGP is to produce the highest quality books — carefully written, immaculately presented and dangerously close to being funny.

Then we work our socks off to get them out to you — at the cheapest possible prices.

C0000 020 140 979

Contents

SECTION 6 — PHONE CALLS AND LETTERS

SECTION 7 — WEATHER, HOLIDAYS AND COUNTRIES

SECTION 8 — GRAMMAR AND PHRASES

Published by CGP

Editors:
Heather Gregson
Rachel Grocott
Sabrina Robinson
Jennifer Underwood

With thanks to Sara Fisher-Stout and Deborah McNee for reviewing this book.

With thanks to Emma Warhurst, Anne Hennessey and Glenda Simpson for the proofreading.

ISBN: 978 1 84762 886 2

Clipart from Corel®
Printed by Elanders Ltd, Newcastle upon Tyne.

Based on the classic CGP style created by Richard Parsons.

Photocopying more than one chapter of this book is not permitted. Extra copies are available from CGP.
0800 1712 712 • www.cgpbooks.co.uk

Numbers

You've got to <u>start somewhere</u>, so why not try something easy, like <u>numbers</u>...

One, two, three — uno, dos, tres...

Numbers are pretty <u>straightforward</u>. After three, <u>let's go</u>...

1-10

1	2	3	4	5	6	7	8	9	10
uno	dos	tres	cuatro	cinco	seis	siete	ocho	nueve	diez

11 to 15 all end in '<u>ce</u>'. But 16, 17, 18 and 19 are '<u>ten and six</u>', etc.

11-19

11	12	13	14	15		16	17	18	19
once	doce	trece	catorce	quince		dieciséis	diecisiete	dieciocho	diecinueve

Most 'ten-type' numbers end in '<u>nta</u>' (except '<u>veinte</u>').

20-100

20	30	40	50	60	70	80	90	100
veinte	treinta	cuarenta	cincuenta	sesenta	setenta	ochenta	noventa	cien

Cien becomes "<u>ciento</u>" when it's followed by another number — e.g. ciento veinte = 120

The in-betweens

21	22	23
veintiuno	veintidós	veintitrés

All <u>twenty-something</u> numbers are rolled into one — "<u>veintiuno</u>" etc.

After <u>30</u>, numbers are joined by "<u>y</u>" (and), but written <u>separately</u> — "<u>treinta y uno</u>" etc.

31	32	33
treinta y uno	treinta y dos	treinta y tres

First, second, third — they're a bit different...

These usually end in "o" for <u>masculine things</u> or "a" for <u>feminine things</u>.

1st — *primero/a* 2nd — *segundo/a* 3rd — *tercero/a* 4th — *cuarto/a* 5th — *quinto/a*

You can always count on numbers...

Ok so numbers aren't exciting but they are <u>useful</u>. If you want <u>exciting</u>, go to Alaska. Brrrr.

Times and Dates

What time is it? Time these Spanish people <u>got a watch</u> and stopped asking, I reckon...

What time is it? — ¿Qué hora es?

If a Spanish person asks you <u>what time it is</u>, you'll be really grateful for this page.

> ¿Qué hora es?   What time is it?

1) Something <u>o'clock</u>:

> *Es la una*
> *It's 1 o'clock*

> *Son las dos*
> *It's 2 o'clock*

This is the <u>tricky bit</u>. If it's 1 o'clock (or to do with 1 o'clock) you say '<u>es la una</u>', but for every other time it's '<u>son</u>'...

2) Something <u>past</u>:

> *Son las dos...*
> *It's...*

> *...y cuarto*
> quarter past two

> *...y media*
> half past two

> *...y veinte*
> twenty past two

3) Something <u>to</u>:

> *Son las tres...*
> *It's...*

> *...menos cuarto*
> quarter to three

> *...menos diez*
> ten to three

When you say '<u>menos</u>', you're saying the hour <u>minus</u> the <u>number of minutes</u>.

To say "<u>at something o'clock</u>", use: **"A las" + TIME**

> *A las seis.*   *At six o'clock.*

'<u>Las</u>' changes to '<u>la</u>' for "<u>a la una</u>" (<u>at one o'clock</u>).

Use 'el' for all the days of the week

Days of the week are all <u>masculine</u>. <u>Don't</u> put capital letters on days.

DAYS OF THE WEEK

lunes	Monday
martes	Tuesday
miércoles	Wednesday
jueves	Thursday
viernes	Friday
sábado	Saturday
domingo	Sunday

WORDS ABOUT THE WEEK

hoy	today
mañana	tomorrow
ayer	yesterday
la semana	week
el fin de semana	weekend
el lunes	on Monday
los lunes	on Mondays

TIMES OF DAY

la mañana	morning	*la tarde*	afternoon / evening	*la noche*	night

There's no time for a clock joke here...

This is <u>basic stuff</u>, but it's <u>important</u>. If you skip the basics you'll get <u>stuck later</u>. And I mean really stuck, like a fly in a vat of <u>sticky toffee pudding</u>. Oh, sticky toffee pudding, how I miss you...

Times and Dates

OK, so next it's... <u>months</u> and <u>dates</u>. Time flies by when you're having fun...

Learn the months of the year

Some Spanish <u>month names</u> are a lot like English ones, but you need to learn how to <u>spell</u> them all.

MR AGOSTO

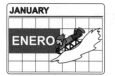
JANUARY — ENERO

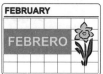
FEBRUARY — FEBRERO

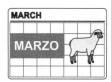
MARCH — MARZO

APRIL — ABRIL

Some useful words:

el día *el mes* *el año*
day   month   year

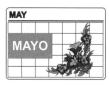
MAY — MAYO

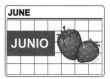
JUNE — JUNIO

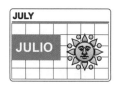
JULY — JULIO

AUGUST — AGOSTO

SEPTEMBER — SEPTIEMBRE

OCTOBER — OCTUBRE

NOVEMBER — NOVIEMBRE

DECEMBER — DICIEMBRE

You say "the 3 of May" instead of "the 3rd of May"

1) In Spanish, they don't say "the <u>third</u> of May" — they say "the <u>three</u> of May".

el tres de mayo   the 3rd of May   ← Months are all <u>masculine</u>. They <u>don't</u> start with capital letters in Spanish.

2) "The <u>first of</u>" is the odd one out:

el primero de mayo   the 1st of May

Check out p.1 for help with the <u>numbers</u>.

3) This is how you <u>write the date</u> in a letter:

5 de enero de 2013   5th of January 2013

4) And to say when your <u>birthday</u> is:

Mi cumpleaños es el trece de septiembre.   My birthday is the 13th of September.

I had a date once — it tasted disgusting...

You won't get far in Spanish if you don't know your <u>months</u>, so get on and <u>learn them</u>. Practise by <u>saying the birthdays of everyone in your family</u> — then you'll have no excuse for forgetting them...

Meeting and Greeting

You need to talk to people in Spanish, and most conversations start with 'hello', so best learn it, I reckon. It's heaps better than just smiling, chewing your lip and saying 'err...'

Hello! — ¡Hola!

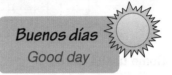

Buenos días
Good day

Buenas tardes
Good afternoon/
Good evening

Buenas noches
Good night

To reply to these, just say the same back.

Goodbye! — ¡Adiós!

Here are three different ways of showing you're leaving:

¡Adiós! Goodbye!   **¡Hasta luego!** See you later!   **¡Hasta pronto!** See you soon!

Learn how to ask how people are

Here's one way to ask how someone is:

¿Qué tal? How are you?

There's another way to ask someone how they are, too.

> See p.7 for more on being formal.

¿Cómo estás? How are you?
For talking to a friend or a family member.

¿Cómo está? How are you?
For talking to an adult or stranger (this version is more formal).

Whichever question you're asked, use this to reply and say how you're feeling:

Bien, gracias. (I am) fine thanks.

> See p.17 if you're not well and you need to explain why.

muy bien   **no muy bien**   **fatal**
very well   not very well   terrible

Goodbye Skegness — hello Marbella...

Now that you've learnt how to greet people (and say bye) and say how you're feeling in Spanish, you're pretty much sorted for those sunkissed holidays on the Costa del Sol. Aaand relaaaax...

Meeting and Greeting

Learn how to <u>introduce</u> people to each other. It's pretty handy at parties and weddings...

Let me introduce Clara — <u>Le presento a Clara</u>

As usual, there's a <u>formal</u> and an <u>informal way</u> to do this. Try the <u>formal way</u> first.

Le presento a mi madre.   *Let me introduce my mother.*

Put any of the <u>people</u> from <u>p.10</u> in here.

Le presento a mi amigo. Se llama George.   *Let me introduce my friend. His name is George.*

You might want to add some details about the person you're introducing.

This is... — <u>Este es / Esta es...</u>

<u>Another way</u> to introduce people is to use '<u>este es</u>' or '<u>esta es</u>'. It's best for <u>informal</u> situations with your friends. Use '<u>este es</u>' for a boy and '<u>esta es</u>' for a girl.

Este es Juan.   *This is Juan.*

Use this one to introduce a <u>boy</u>.

Esta es Sara.   *This is Sara.*

Use this one to introduce a <u>girl</u>.

Pleased to meet you — <u>Mucho Gusto</u>

Unfortunately, if I tried to shake your hand, my trousers would fall down.

Now you've been introduced you need <u>something else</u> to say...

There are a few ways to say '<u>pleased to meet you</u>':

Mucho gusto.   *Pleased to meet you.*

Encanta<u>do</u>.   *Pleased to meet you.*

Use this one if <u>you're a boy</u>.

Encanta<u>da</u>.   *Pleased to meet you.*

Use this one if <u>you're a girl</u>.

When people are talking to each other in <u>formal situations</u> you might hear them say '<u>señor</u>' or '<u>señora</u>'.

Encantada, señor.   *Pleased to meet you, sir.*

Encantado

señora *madam*

Spanish weather forecast — mucho gusto...

It's tricky using <u>different word endings</u> for <u>girls</u> and <u>boys</u> in Spanish, when you're not used to doing it in English. Once you've practised it a few times you'll <u>soon get the hang of it</u> though.

Being Polite

Here's the <u>first rule</u> for learning any foreign language — if you can only say <u>two things</u>, they should be '<u>please</u>' and '<u>thank you</u>'. You can get quite a long way with those...

Please — *por favor*, thank you — *gracías*

1) Learn how to say "<u>please</u>" and "<u>thank you</u>":

por favor please	*gracias* thank you
muchas gracias thank you very much	

2) If someone says "thank you", say "<u>you're welcome</u>":

de nada you're welcome

yes **SÍ**   no **NO**

You won't get <u>far</u> without these <u>little beauties</u>...

I'm sorry — *Lo siento*

If you <u>never</u> do anything you might have to <u>apologise</u> for, you can skip this bit... as if.

lo siento I'm sorry	*lo siento mucho* I'm really sorry

Excuse me — *Perdone*

There are <u>different types</u> of '<u>excuse me</u>' you need to know.

ASKING SOMETHING

This is what you say if you want to <u>ask the way</u>, or attract someone's <u>attention</u>.

¡Perdone, señora! Excuse me, madam!

¡Por favor! Excuse me!

señor sir

MOVING SOMEONE

This is what you say if someone's <u>in the way</u>, and you want to get past.

¡Con permiso! Excuse me!

Now you can push people out of the way internationally...

In some countries, people don't say '<u>excuse me</u>' and '<u>please</u>' as much as we do in the UK. They're not ruder — it's just <u>different cultures</u>. No one loves a queue quite as much as the UK, either...

Being Polite

This bit is jolly useful. Learn how to <u>say what you want</u>.

I would like — Quisiera

It's much more polite to say '<u>quisiera</u>' (I would like) than '<u>quiero</u>' (I want).

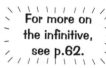

1) Here's how to say you would like <u>something</u>:

> *Quisiera <u>un zumo de naranja</u>.*   *I would like <u>an orange juice</u>.*

2) Here's how to say you would like <u>to do</u> something:

> *"Quisiera" + INFINITIVE* → *Quisiera <u>hablar</u>.*   *I would like <u>to talk</u>.*

The verb needs to be in the <u>infinitive form</u>.   The infinitive

> For more on
> the infinitive,
> see p.62.

May I...? — ¿Puedo...?

A useful way of asking for things is to use '<u>puedo</u>'.

> *¿"Puedo" + INFINITIVE ?* → *¿Puedo <u>ir</u> al baño?*   *May I <u>go</u> to the toilet?*

Exactly the same here — the verb needs
to be in the <u>infinitive form</u>.   The infinitive

<u>*And a little bit about the <u>polite 'you'</u> in Spanish...*</u>

If you want to be <u>extra polite</u> in Spanish, there's a <u>formal</u> way of saying '<u>you</u>'.

1) Spanish people use the <u>informal</u> 'you' for talking to a <u>friend</u> or <u>family member</u>:

> *¿Qué <u>quieres</u> comer?*   *What do <u>you want</u> to eat?*

Informal '<u>you</u>'.

2) They use the <u>polite</u> 'you' for someone they <u>don't know well</u>, e.g. a <u>hotel receptionist</u>:

> *¿Qué <u>quiere</u> comer?*   *What do <u>you want</u> to eat?*

For more on '<u>you singular</u>'
and '<u>he/she/it</u>' verb forms,
see <u>p.62-70</u>.

<u>Polite '<u>you</u>'</u> — this 'you' follows the <u>same pattern</u> as the '<u>he/she/it</u>' form of the verb.

You'll come across the <u>polite</u> '<u>you</u>' on pages about <u>booking a hotel room</u> or <u>going to the doctor</u>.

I want never gets...

Learn how to <u>recognise</u> the <u>polite 'you'</u> and when it's used. Just remember, if you don't know the person, it's better to <u>be polite</u>, just in case they like <u>eating impolite teenagers for breakfast</u>...

Summary Questions

Ah, it's time for my favourite part... I get to ask you loads of questions on the section you've just read, and you get to answer them. All the answers you need are in the section though, so if you're stuck, just look back at the relevant page to help you. It might look like a lot of questions, but they're really quick to do, honest. Go through them, check your answers are right, and if they're not, go back and do them again...

1) How do you say these numbers in Spanish?
   a) 13   b) 28   c) 39   d) 77   e) 100

2) How do you say 'third' in Spanish? (Give the masculine and feminine version.)

3) How do you say "What time is it?" in Spanish?

4) You ask a Mexican the time and he says "Son las tres y media". What time is it?

5) How do you say "It's twenty past four" in Spanish?

6) You ask your friend Lola when she normally goes to the sports centre. She says "Voy los viernes". Which day does she go?

7) How do you say 'tomorrow' in Spanish? (Don't forget the accent.)

8) What is 'Sunday' in Spanish?

9) Write down the month you were born in Spanish.

10) You ask your friend when his birthday is, and he replies "El doce de agosto." When is it?

11) Write down today's date as if you were putting it in a letter.

12) How would you say hello in the following situations? (Don't use ¡Hola!)
    a) in the morning   b) at night   c) in the evening

13) Your friend Puri says "¡Hasta pronto!". What is she saying?

14) Your Spanish friend has just introduced you to their brother, Javier. How would you say "pleased to meet you" in Spanish? Write down two ways of saying this.

15) Your friend Miguel says "¿Qué tal?" Tell him in Spanish that you feel terrible.

16) You ask Miguel how he is and he says "Muy bien". What is he saying?

17) How would you say "you're welcome" in Spanish?

18) Now Miguel is saying "Lo siento mucho". What does he mean?

19) You want to ask someone the way in Granada. How do you attract their attention?

20) How do you say "I would like to go to the cinema" in Spanish?

Your Details

Me, myself and I. My three favourite topics of conversation...

Me llamo Paco. Me gusta nadar...

Talking about yourself — facts and figures

You need to know how to ask and answer these questions.
Change the highlighted words to answer about yourself.

¿Cómo te llamas?   What are you called?

Me llamo Lola.   I'm called Lola.

¿Cuántos años tienes?   How old are you?

Tengo trece años.   I'm thirteen.

¿Cuándo es tu cumpleaños?
When is your birthday?

Mi cumpleaños es el cuatro de octubre.
My birthday is the 4th of October.

For more numbers and dates, see p.1 and 3.

¿Qué te gusta?   What do you like?

Me gusta el tenis.   I like tennis.

Say what you look like

Learn how to say what you look like. But remember, beauty is only skin deep...

Soy alto/a.   I am tall.

slim:	delgado/a	medium height:	de talla mediana
fat:	gordo/a	short (in height):	bajo/a

Tengo los ojos marrones.   I have brown eyes.

green: verdes   blue: azules

Use the '-o' endings if you're a boy and the '-a' endings if you're a girl.

Tengo el pelo largo.   I have long hair.

black:	negro	very short:	muy corto
brown:	castaño	quite long:	bastante largo
blonde:	rubio		

Llevo gafas.   I wear glasses.
No llevo gafas.   I don't wear glasses.

Soy pelirrojo/a.
I have red hair.

Soy trabajador.

Describe your personality

'Deportista' ends in an 'a' for boys and girls.

Soy...	simpático/a	nice	perezoso/a	lazy	inteligente	intelligent
I am...	tímido/a	shy	deportista	sporty	trabajador(a)	hardworking

I hate those people who just talk about themselves...

Actually, I'm one of those people. But you need to be able to ask other people about themselves if you want to make lots of Spanish-speaking friends — which I know you do, so get practising...

Your Family

You can choose your <u>friends</u> but you can't choose your <u>family</u> — just like you can't avoid this <u>vocab</u> at KS3. This page will help you to <u>talk</u> about them, whatever you think of them...

Use these words for your friends and family

mi padre — my father
mi madre — my mother
mi padrastro — my stepfather
mi madrastra — my stepmother

mi primo — my cousin (male)
mi prima — my cousin (female)
mi tía — my aunt
mi tío — my uncle

mi hermana — my sister
mi hermano — my brother
mi hermanastra — my stepsister
mi hermanastro — my stepbrother

mi abuela — my grandmother
mi abuelo — my grandfather

mi amigo — my friend (male)
mi amiga — my friend (female)

Say what your family and friends are like

Some words change for <u>girls</u> or <u>boys</u>. Take a little look at the sentences below to see how. I've <u>underlined</u> the bits that change. Handy.

BOYS

Tengo <u>un</u> herman<u>o</u>. *I have a brother.*

Mi herman<u>o</u> se llama David.
My brother is called David.

<u>Él</u> tiene dieciséis años.
He is sixteen years old.

<u>Él</u> es simpátic<u>o</u>. *He is nice.*

If you're an only child, you say:
'Soy hijo único' (boys)
'Soy hija única' (girls)

GIRLS

Tengo <u>una</u> herman<u>a</u>. *I have a sister.*

Mi herman<u>a</u> se llama Luisa.
My sister is called Luisa.

<u>Ella</u> tiene diez años.
She is ten years old.

<u>Ella</u> es simpátic<u>a</u>. *She is nice.*

My family is like a fruit cake — sweet, but a bit nutty...

Make sure you get your <u>endings</u> right for family members. Remember '<u>-a</u>' endings are <u>feminine</u> and '<u>-o</u>' endings are <u>masculine</u>. You don't want a Spanish person to think you have an uncle Sandra...

Pets and Animals

Animals are much nicer than people. Except my sister's hamster, which bites.
Whether you've got pets or not, it's useful to know animal names.

Learn the animals — *Los animales*

Oh yes, and don't forget to learn if they go with '<u>un</u>' or '<u>una</u>'.

un perro *a dog*	**un conejo** *a rabbit*	**un gato** *a cat*	**un ratón** *a mouse*
un hámster *a hamster*	**un pájaro** *a bird*	**una tortuga** *a tortoise*	**un caballo** *a horse*

I have a cat — *Tengo un gato*

Learn how to have a chat about pets. Change "gato" so it's about your pet.

1)
> ¿Tienes animales en casa?
> *Do you have any pets?*

Another word for pet is 'mascota'.

2)
> No tengo animales en casa.
> *I don't have any pets.*

3)
> Tengo un gato. *I have a cat.*

4)
> Mi gato se llama Alfie.
> *My cat is called Alfie.*

See p.32 for colours.

5)

Mi gato es		
My cat is	gordo/a	fat
	negro/a	black
	bonito/a	pretty
	feo/a	ugly

My cat swallowed a duck — now he's a duck-filled fatty-puss...

If you <u>don't</u> have any pets to talk about, make <u>something</u> up. Use a dictionary to pick your dream pet and all its <u>weird</u> and <u>wonderful</u> traits. E.g. "I have an African elephant shrew called Lawrence..."

Your Home

This page wants you to make yourself at <u>home</u> and learn all this lovely <u>vocab</u>...

Talk about the <u>rooms</u> in your house — *Las habitaciones*

el salón
living room

el comedor
dining room

el dormitorio
bedroom

el cuarto de baño
bathroom

la cocina
kitchen

el jardín
garden

In my house — *En mi casa*

> See p.60 for 'my', 'your' etc.

It's useful to learn that '<u>mi</u> casa' means '<u>my</u> house' and '<u>tu</u> casa' means '<u>your</u> house'.

¿Qué hay en tu casa?
What is there in your house?

En mi casa hay cinco habitaciones.
In my house there are five rooms.

En mi casa hay un salón, una cocina y dos dormitorios.
In my house there is a living room, a kitchen and two bedrooms.

> Change the bits in the white boxes to make sentences about your own home.

Talk about the <u>furniture</u> — *Los muebles*

And it wouldn't be a home without <u>furniture</u>. Think about it. It would just be weird.

un armario
wardrobe

un sofá
sofa

una silla
chair

un sillón
armchair

una mesa
table

una cama
bed

In your room — *En tu dormitorio*

Yup, another set of <u>questions</u> and <u>answers</u> you need to learn. Hard luck.
Remember that to say '<u>a</u>' in Spanish, '<u>el</u>' changes to '<u>un</u>' and '<u>la</u>' changes to '<u>una</u>.'

QUESTION

¿Qué hay en tu dormitorio?
What is there in your room?

ANSWER

Hay una cama, un armario y una mesa.
There is a bed, a wardrobe and a table.

KS3 Study Guides — good for wedging under wobbly table legs...

Actually, this one's pretty good for learning Spanish, too. Cover up the <u>labels</u> under the pictures and <u>test</u> yourself. Soon you'll be so <u>good</u>, you could recite the entire IKEA catalogue in Spanish...

Where You Live

Home is where the <u>heart</u> is. An Englishman's home is his <u>castle</u>. There's no place like <u>home</u>...

Where do you live? — ¿Dónde vives?

Learn the names of <u>types of home</u>...

Vivo en ...
I live in ...

una casa
a house

un apartamento
a flat

una granja
a farm

... and the words for <u>where you live</u>.

Vivo en ...
I live in ...

un pueblo
a village

una ciudad
a town / a city

VALUE ADDED EXTRAS

Vivo en el campo.
I live in the countryside.

Vivo en las montañas.
I live in the mountains.

Vivo cerca del mar.
I live near the sea.

Then string together <u>a sentence</u> you can use <u>again</u> and <u>again</u>.

I live in York, a city in the north of England.

Vivo en York, una ciudad en el norte de Inglaterra.

Put the name of the place where you live here.

una ciudad a town / a city
un pueblo a village

Pick the right description using the compass diagram.

del país de Gales of Wales
de Escocia of Scotland
de Irlanda del Norte of Northern Ireland

Compass Points

el norte the north
el noroeste the north-west
el noreste the north-east
el oeste the west
el este the east
el suroeste the south-west
el sureste the south-east
el sur the south

Do you like living here? — ¿Te gusta vivir aquí?

Me gusta vivir aquí...
I like living here...

porque es...
because it is...

tranquilo	peaceful
limpio	clean
estupendo	great

No me gusta vivir aquí...
I don't like living here...

porque es...
because it is...

aburrido	boring
sucio	dirty
horrible	horrible

There was an old woman who lived in a shoe...

If you're <u>directly</u> describing the place where you live, the describing words have to <u>change</u> to match. So, 'Mi pueblo es <u>limpio</u>' but 'Mi ciudad es <u>limpia</u>'. Fiddly, I know. But you'll get there.

Daily Routine

You might find this a bit... <u>routine</u>. But I bet you this kind of vocab will come in handy.

Daily routine — *Say what you do*

'Me' + a verb usually means the verb is reflexive. See p.66 for an explanation.

Me despierto. *I wake up.*   **Me levanto.** *I get up.*

Me lavo. *I get washed.*   **Me lavo los dientes.** *I brush my teeth.*

Me visto. *I get dressed.*

Desayuno. *I eat breakfast.*

Voy al instituto. *I go to school.*

Vuelvo a casa. *I come back home.*

Hago mis deberes. *I do my homework.*

Veo la televisión. *I watch T.V.*

Ceno. *I have dinner.*

Me acuesto. *I go to bed.*

Say when you do it — *A las*

See p.2 for how to tell the time.

Adding in the <u>time</u> of day is a great way to <u>improve</u> phrases about your daily routine.

activity + time

Me levanto <u>a las siete</u>.   I get up <u>at seven</u>.
Vuelvo a casa <u>a las cuatro</u>.   I come back home <u>at four</u>.
Ceno <u>a las seis y media</u>.   I have dinner <u>at half past six</u>.
Me acuesto <u>a las nueve</u>.   I go to bed <u>at nine</u>.

Woke up, fell out of bed, dragged a comb across my head...

These are the basic <u>phrases</u> that you really do <u>need</u> to know at KS3. No escaping them. Sorry...

Chores

Here's a bunch of <u>chores</u> that you might have to do at home. If you <u>don't</u> do any chores at home — lucky you. But you still need to <u>learn</u> them for KS3 Spanish...

Do you help at home? — ¿Ayudas en casa?

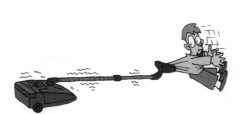

Paso la aspiradora.

I do the vacuum cleaning.

Lavo los platos.

I wash the dishes.

Lavo el coche.

I wash the car.

Limpio la casa.

I clean the house.

Arreglo mi dormitorio.

I tidy my room.

Pongo la mesa.

I lay the table.

Hago mi cama.

I make my bed.

Hago la compra.

I do the shopping.

No hago nada.

I don't do anything.

Learning chores — what a chore...

You're right — that's quite a lot of <u>vocab</u>. Not to mention the fact that the thought of <u>tidying</u> my room is enough to make me feel slightly sick... I know. Let's have a <u>biscuit</u>. Much better.

The Body

Body parts are really useful, especially if you're ill or if you hurt something... (See the next page).

The head — La cabeza

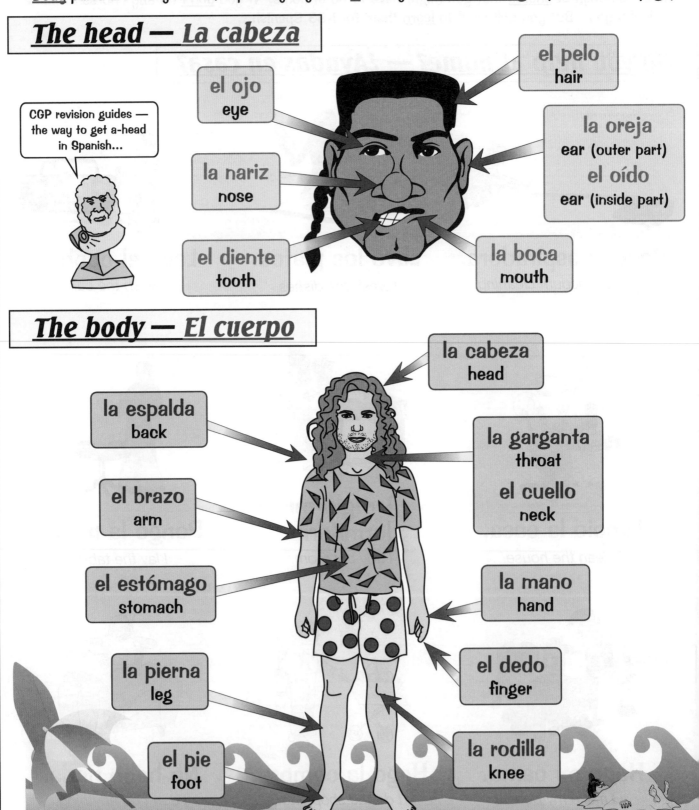

el pelo — hair

el ojo — eye

la oreja — ear (outer part)
el oído — ear (inside part)

la nariz — nose

el diente — tooth

la boca — mouth

CGP revision guides — the way to get a-head in Spanish...

The body — El cuerpo

la cabeza — head

la espalda — back

la garganta — throat
el cuello — neck

el brazo — arm

el estómago — stomach

la mano — hand

la pierna — leg

el dedo — finger

el pie — foot

la rodilla — knee

You stick your left leg in, your left leg out...

This page is simply begging you to cover the labels and test yourself on the vocab. That's really all this page wants. You would make its day if you did that. And you would learn loads too...

Health and Illness

It's horrible when you feel <u>ill</u>, and even worse if you're supposed to be on holiday.
At least with this handy <u>vocab</u>, you could get a Spanish <u>doctor</u> to fix you up <u>ASAP</u>...

Tell someone you're ill — *"Estoy enfermo/a"*

Estoy enfermo/a.			
I am ill.			

Quiero ir...	...al médico.	...a la farmacia.	...al hospital.
I want to go...	*...to the doctor's.*	*...to the pharmacy.*	*...to the hospital.*

My 🩹 hurts — *Me duele el / la* 🩹

Being able to explain what <u>hurts</u> is important. It's also good <u>practice</u> for the body parts on p.16.

"Me duele" + "el / la" + BODY PART ➡️

Me duele el estómago.   *My stomach hurts.*

Me duele la cabeza.   *My head hurts. (I have a headache).*

Me duele la espalda.   *My back hurts.*

If you're using a <u>plural</u>, the verb '<u>duele</u>' needs to change to '<u>duelen</u>' to match:

"Me duelen" + "los / las" + BODY PARTS ➡️

Me duelen los pies.   *My feet hurt.*

Me duelen las piernas.   *My legs hurt.*

And here's <u>another</u> useful sentence:

Tengo gripe.   *I've got flu.*

See <u>p.56</u> for more about '<u>el</u>', '<u>la</u>', '<u>los</u>' and '<u>las</u>'.

Learn these things for making you better

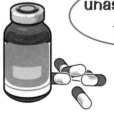

unas pastillas
tablets

una receta
a prescription

un jarabe
a syrup

una tirita
a plaster

una crema
a cream

Vocab for illness — it's a pain in the neck...

Even if you're as <u>fit</u> as a butcher's dog, you need to <u>learn</u> this vocab for KS3. On the bright side, it's not very often you get to practise <u>complaining</u> about how awful you feel. You might enjoy it...

Summary Questions

After that fabulous section about you, your family and your home, here are some fabulous practice questions to go with it. (Don't pull that face.) Answer them, correct the mistakes, and answer them again until you get them all right. You'll be un/a experto/a in no time...

1) How would you ask me what my name is in Spanish?

2) Answer these questions in Spanish: a) ¿Cuántos años tienes?
                                      b) ¿Cuándo es tu cumpleaños?

3) Describe what you look like in Spanish. Mention at least four things.

4) What do these words mean in English? a) tímido   b) perezoso   c) simpático

5) Write these words in Spanish:
   a) my grandmother   b) my brother   c) my uncle   d) my cousin (female)

6) Write these sentences in Spanish: "I have a sister. She has blonde hair. She is hardworking."

7) In Spanish, how do you ask someone if they have any pets?

8) What are these animals in Spanish?
   a) a mouse   b) a horse   c) a bird
   d) a rabbit   e) a dog   f) a duck-billed platypus*

9) Write down what these words mean in English:
   a) el cuarto de baño   b) la cocina   c) el comedor   d) el jardín

10) In Spanish, answer the question "¿Qúe hay en tu dormitorio?"

11) Río and Luis live in the same town. Río likes living there because it's clean. Luis doesn't like living there because it's boring. Write out what they would say about their town in Spanish.

12) Write in Spanish: "I live in Dover, a town in the south-east of England."

13) Write what these mean in English:
    a) Desayuno.   b) Me acuesto.   c) Hago mis deberes.   d) Me levanto.

14) Write out your personal daily routine, including the time you do things.

15) How do you ask someone if they help at home in Spanish?

16) List five chores that you might do to help at home.

17) In Spanish, write labels for the two diagrams labelled a-g.

18) Andreas says "Me duele la espalda." What's wrong with him?

19) List three things in Spanish that you might buy from the pharmacy if you're unwell.

20) How would you tell a Spanish person that you're ill and want to go to the doctor's?

*(Only joking...)

School Subjects

What could be better than talking <u>about school</u> in Spanish <u>at school</u>...
Being able to say which <u>subjects</u> you <u>love</u> (and <u>hate</u>) is one of teachers' favourite subjects.

School subjects — Las asignaturas

Knowing your subjects is really important so learn <u>all</u> of them — even those you <u>don't</u> study.

SCIENCES

las ciencias	science
la física	physics
la química	chemistry
la biología	biology

LANGUAGES

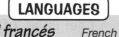

el francés	French
el alemán	German
el español	Spanish
el inglés	English

ART AND MUSIC

| el dibujo | art |
| la música | music |

NUMBERS AND STUFF

| las matemáticas | maths |
| la informática | IT |

HUMANITIES

la historia	history
la geografía	geography
la religión	religious studies

PHYSICAL EDUCATION

| la educación física | PE |

You don't need the '<u>el</u>' or '<u>la</u>' when you say what you study.

This is how to say what you do:
(Just change 'español' to any other subject)

Estudio <u>español</u>.

My favourite subject — Mi asignatura preferida

Tell everyone <u>what you think</u> about your <u>favourite</u> (and <u>least favourite</u>) subjects.

"Mi asignatura preferida es" + subject → Mi asignatura preferida es la geografía.
My favourite subject is geography.

<u>Me gusta</u> la biología. *I like biology.*

When you talk about a subject that's <u>plural</u>, like maths, '<u>me gusta</u>' changes to '<u>me gustan</u>'.

Odio la historia. *I hate history.*

porque es... *because it's...*

And this is how you'd say why:

| interesante: interesting | fácil: easy | útil: useful |
| aburrido: boring | difícil: difficult | inútil: pointless |

I like all subjects — yeah right...

There are loads of subjects to learn here. <u>Learn them in groups</u> to make it easier for you. And once you've learnt them, you may as well learn how to say <u>why</u> you like them or hate them. Fun stuff.

School Routine

You must know your <u>school routine</u> off by heart by now — you spend enough time there. Sigh. This page is about <u>getting to school</u> and <u>what you do</u> when you get there.

The school day — La jornada escolar

Writing about your <u>school day</u> in Spanish — not the most fun you'll ever have but it's <u>important</u>.

Me levanto a las siete. = I get up at 7:00.

For more on daily routine, see <u>p.14</u>.

Voy al instituto *I go to school*

- *en coche* by car
- *a pie* on foot
- *en autobús* by bus
- *en bicicleta* by bike

→ **Voy al instituto en bicicleta.** = I go to school by bike.

Las clases empiezan a *las nueve*. = Lessons start at 9:00.

Las clases terminan a *las tres y media*. = Lessons end at 3:30.

For more on times, see <u>p.2</u>.

Cada clase dura *cuarenta minutos*. = Each lesson lasts 40 minutes.

Tenemos *ocho* clases por día. = We have 8 lessons per day.

Hacemos *una hora* de deberes por día. = We do one hour of homework per day.

For more on numbers, see <u>p.1</u>.

A pie — great, I'm starving...

Unfortunately, this page is less exciting than eating pies, but it's always useful to be able to <u>talk about your school day</u>. <u>Time</u> and <u>transport</u> are really <u>handy</u> for loads of <u>other topics</u> too — hurrah.

Classroom Stuff

Oddly enough, Spanish teachers like to <u>talk</u> in <u>Spanish</u>. That's why this page is really helpful for <u>understanding</u> them. If you hear '<u>silencio</u>', it means they're about to start rabbiting on again...

Silence! — ¡Silencio!

Make sure you know what your <u>teacher's</u> saying. That'll <u>impress</u> 'em.

For more on commands, see <u>p.69</u>.

Stand up! = | ¡Levántate! | ← *For talking to <u>one person</u>.* → | ¡Siéntate! | = Sit down!
| ¡Levantaos! | ← *For talking to <u>more than one person</u>.* → | ¡Sentaos! |

You might hear these in the <u>classroom</u> too...

¿Qué quiere decir eso? = What does that mean?

¿Cómo se dice en <u>español</u>? = How do you say it in <u>Spanish</u>?

¿Cómo se dice en <u>inglés</u>? = How do you say it in <u>English</u>?

¡Silencio! = Silence!

Verdadero = True

Falso = False

In the classroom — En el aula

You have to admit, '<u>un bolígrafo</u>' sounds <u>way more interesting</u> than just a plain old '<u>pen</u>'...

un bolígrafo — a pen

una goma — a rubber

un lápiz — a pencil

una regla — a ruler

'un alumno' for a boy

una alumna — a pupil (girl)

¡Levantaos!

'una profesora' for a woman

un profesor — a teacher (man)

una clase — a lesson

un uniforme — a uniform

un libro — a book

un horario — a timetable

un cuaderno — an exercise book

Quisiera un bolígrafo, una goma, un lápiz, un libro y una regla...

Your teacher will get annoyed if you want to empty the <u>whole</u> stationery cupboard but "<u>quisiera un bolígrafo</u>" (I'd like a pen) is useful for trying to get on their good side when you've forgotten yours.

Jobs

Learn this job vocab. You might have to answer questions about <u>which job you'd like</u> to do and what your <u>family</u> does. Even if you've <u>not got a clue</u> about the future, just <u>make something up</u>.

Lots of jobs — *Muchos trabajos*   [el trabajo = job]

In Spanish, the word for a job can depend on <u>who's doing it</u>. The 🚹 words are for <u>men</u> and the 🚺 words are for <u>women</u>. 🚻 means it's the same word for <u>both men and women</u>.

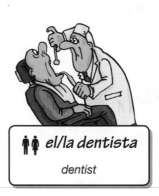

🚻 el/la dentista

dentist

🚹 el médico
🚺 la médica

doctor

🚹 el enfermero
🚺 la enfermera

nurse

🚹 el peluquero
🚺 la peluquera

hairdresser

🚻 el/la albañil

builder

🚹 el ingeniero
🚺 la ingeniera

engineer

🚹 el mecánico
🚺 la mecánica

mechanic

🚻 el/la policía

police officer

🚹 el vendedor
🚺 la vendedora

salesperson

🚹 el profesor
🚺 la profesora

teacher

🚹 el actor
🚺 la actriz

actor

🚹 el secretario
🚺 la secretaria

secretary

Revising KS3 Spanish — it's all work work work...

Talking about <u>jobs</u> is <u>super useful stuff</u> so make sure you learn all the job words on this page (plus the male and female versions). Put it all into <u>practice</u> on the next page. You know you want to...

Talking About Jobs

You might not know <u>what you want to be</u> when you're older. You might know exactly what you're going to do. Whatever, you need to know how to <u>say what you and other people do</u>. Here goes...

Say what *you* and *other people* do

If you've got a job, learn to say <u>what you do</u>. Learn how to say what <u>your parents do</u> too.

Soy estudiante.
I am a student.

Trabajo a tiempo parcial.
I work part-time.

Mi padre es policía.
My father is a police officer.

Reparto periódicos.
I deliver newspapers.

Trabajo en 'Pets R us'.
I work at 'Pets R us'.

You don't need 'un' or 'una' when you're talking about what jobs people do.

"Soy" + JOB → *Soy dentista.* I'm a dentist.

Mi madre es profesora.
My mother is a teacher.

Say what *you want* to do — "*Quiero ser*"

Say what you want to <u>study</u> (for GCSEs or A-levels, for example) like this:

"Quiero estudiar" + SUBJECT → *Quiero estudiar biología* I want to study biology

Don't forget to give a <u>reason</u>:

Brenda dahling, I've told you a hundred times, yah. Subjects are on <u>page 19</u>...

...porque
...because

es interesante it's interesting

es útil it's useful

es divertido/a it's fun

es fácil it's easy

quiero ser enfermero/a I want to be a nurse

Say what you want to <u>be</u> like this:

"Quiero ser" + JOB → *Quiero ser actor.*
I want to be an actor.

You can replace these with any of the jobs from <u>p.22</u>.

Give a <u>reason</u> — you can use the reasons above, or this one's good too:

Quiero ser médico porque ganan mucho dinero.
I want to be a doctor because they earn a lot of money.

Quiero ser rico y famoso...

This page is great for practising everything you've already learnt about <u>subjects</u> and <u>jobs</u>. Learn to say <u>what you and your family do</u>, and <u>what you want to study</u>, and you won't go far wrong.

Summary Questions

I've got some good news and some bad news. The bad news is, you've got a page of questions to do but the good news is, you'll have earned yourself a cup of tea by the end of it. And if you get them all right first time round, I'd say you deserve a choccy biscuit to dunk in it. So the deal is, answer all of these questions, look up any answers you don't know, then try again. And make sure you've got them all right before you hit that kettle switch. I mean it — I've got my eye on you...

1) Write a sentence in Spanish for each subject you study, starting with 'Estudio'.

2) Which subjects do you like? Which do you hate? Answer in Spanish, in full sentences, and don't forget to give a reason for each one.

3) In Spanish, write down how you get to school.

4) How do you say that you have six lessons per day?

5) How long is each lesson at your school? Write it down in Spanish — make sure you write the number out in full too.

6) Write down that you do two hours of homework per day. In Spanish, obviously.

7) If you hear your teacher shouting these, what are they telling you to do?
   a) ¡Sentaos!   b) ¡Silencio!   c) ¡Levantaos!

8) Write down how to say 'true' and 'false' in Spanish.

9) Your teacher points at a pen and says "¿Cómo se dice en español?". What would you say?

10) Your teacher just loves speaking Spanish. She says "¿Cómo se dice "un cuaderno" en inglés?". What would your answer be?

11) Write down the names in Spanish for:
    a) a pencil   b) a ruler   c) a timetable   d) a uniform

12) What are these in English?
    a) un profesor   b) un libro   c) una goma   d) un alumno

13) What are these jobs in Spanish? (Give the male and female versions, including 'el' and 'la'.)
    a) doctor   b) teacher   c) hairdresser   d) nurse   e) actor

14) Write down what job you want to do. Say what jobs your parents do too.

15) How would you say that you work part-time at 'RapidBurgerz'?

16) Write in Spanish:
    "I want to study IT because it's useful. I want to be an engineer because it's interesting."

17) What does this mean? "Quiero estudiar español porque es divertido."

18) Write down this sentence in Spanish: "I want to be a salesperson because it's easy."

Directions

This page helps you <u>get to</u> the shops. Pick me up <u>a packet of biscuits</u> while you're there...

Where is... ? — ¿Dónde está... ?

There are <u>two</u> questions you can ask to <u>find your way</u> somewhere — you need to know <u>both</u> of them. (Sorry.)

Replace with any place from p.26-27. Use "al" for "el" words and "a la" for "la" words — they both mean "to the".

¿Dónde está la estación ?
Where's <u>the station</u>?

¿Para ir al banco ?
How do I get <u>to the bank</u>?

¿Para ir al banco?

UNDERSTANDING DIRECTIONS

Gire a la izquierda
Turn left

Siga todo recto
Go straight on

Gire a la derecha
Turn right

**Tome la primera calle
a la izquierda / derecha**
Take the first road on the left / right

**Tome la segunda calle
a la izquierda / derecha**
Take the second road on the left / right

Is it far from here? — ¿Está lejos de aquí?

If the place you're looking for is <u>miles away</u>, you don't just want to set off walking there.

¿Está lejos de aquí?   *Is it far from here?*

Está lejos.
It's <u>far away</u>.

Está cerca.
It's <u>nearby</u>.

Está a dos kilómetros.
It's <u>two kilometres away</u>.

Get the bus? Don't be ridiculous...

Quick, take me to the nearest fast-food restaurant...

Sometimes there's a moment when only lumps of bony chicken in a soggy batter coating will do. If you <u>don't understand directions</u>, you'll <u>never</u> make it to a Spanish outlet of 'Chicken Bits R Us'...

Shops

Now you know how to ask for directions, it's time to learn some <u>places to go</u>.

Shops — Las tiendas

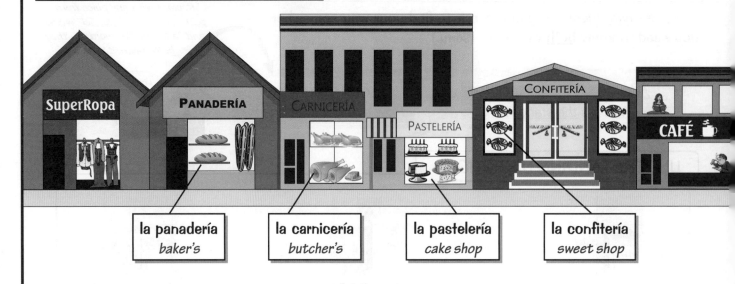

la panadería	la carnicería	la pastelería	la confitería
baker's	*butcher's*	*cake shop*	*sweet shop*

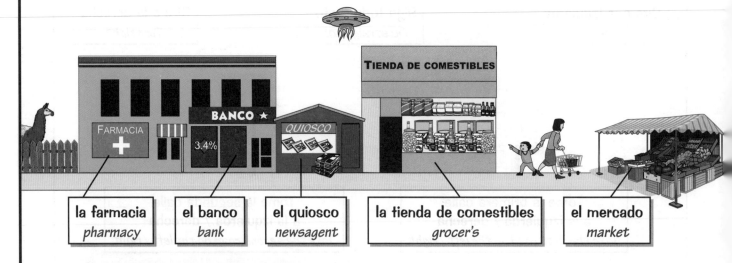

la farmacia	el banco	el quiosco	la tienda de comestibles	el mercado
pharmacy	*bank*	*newsagent*	*grocer's*	*market*

Places where you'll find books

It's easy to get these <u>mixed up</u> — 'la librería' means <u>bookshop</u> and 'la biblioteca' means <u>library</u>.

la librería	la biblioteca
bookshop	*library*

This page just wouldn't be complete without a place to buy <u>everything</u>...

el supermercado
supermarket

Maybe 'supermercado' is the only one you need...

Words, words, words... these pages are so <u>full of words</u> you can find yourself longing for <u>complete</u> <u>sentences</u> after a while. But fear not, there are <u>plenty</u> more of those to come. Just keep going...

Places in Town

This is basic 'learn-it-or-else' vocab. "Or else what?" you may ask. Well, you'll get no better at Spanish...

Learn all these places

la estación (de trenes)
the railway station

Correos
the post office

'Correos' is masculine but it's not used with the article — it just stays as 'Correos'.

la iglesia
the church

el teatro
the theatre

el museo
the museum

el cine
the cinema

el polideportivo
the leisure centre

el parque
the park

el castillo
the castle

la oficina de turismo
the tourist office

el hotel
the hotel

la piscina
the swimming pool

el ayuntamiento
the town hall

el hospital
the hospital

No games arcades or mobile phone shops then...

The types of building they expect you to learn do confuse me a bit. I bet you've never needed to know where the town hall is in the UK, so why would you want to know in Spain? Hmm.

Food and Drink

This is my favourite bit — it's all about things to <u>eat and drink</u>.

Fruit — Las frutas

la pera
pear

la manzana
apple

el plátano
banana

el limón
lemon

la naranja
orange

la fresa
strawberry

el melocotón
peach

Vegetables — Las verduras

la patata
potato

la zanahoria
carrot

el tomate
tomato

el champiñón
mushroom

los guisantes
peas

la cebolla
onion

la coliflor
cauliflower

la judía
bean

la lechuga
lettuce

Meat — La carne

el filete
steak

la hamburguesa
burger

la carne de vaca
beef

el pollo
chicken

la carne de cerdo
pork

el cordero
lamb

la salchicha
sausage

el jamón
ham

el pescado
fish

los mariscos
seafood, shellfish

This page is making me hungry...

This food vocab comes up <u>all the time</u>. It might seem boring, but you've just got to <u>learn it</u>. If you don't, you'll have to eat at the places with photos of food on the menus, and they're <u>really terrible</u>.

Food and Drink

This page is a bit <u>mix and match</u> — sweet stuff, dairy, other random food and drink...

Desserts — Los postres

Not just desserts — there's <u>other sweet stuff</u> too.

el helado
ice cream

la galleta
biscuit

la tarta / el pastel
cake

el chocolate
chocolate

el azúcar
sugar

la mermelada
jam

DAIRY STUFF

la nata	cream
el queso	cheese
el yogur	yoghurt
la leche	milk
el huevo	egg
la mantequilla	butter

Drinks — Las bebidas

HOT DRINKS

el té
tea

el café (con leche)
coffee (with milk)

el chocolate caliente
hot chocolate

la sopa*
soup

*Not technically a drink, but it's hot and liquidy...

ALCOHOL

la cerveza
beer

el vino tinto
red wine

el vino blanco
white wine

OTHER DRINKS

el agua mineral
mineral water

la limonada
lemonade

Stick in <u>any fruit</u> from p.28
to make <u>any juice</u>.

el zumo/jugo de <u>naranja</u>
orange juice

Other Tasty Stuff

Mmm — bring on the <u>carbs</u>.

el pan
bread

los cereales
cereal

las patatas fritas
chips

el bocadillo
sandwich

la pasta
pasta

el arroz
rice

Mermelada — confusingly not always marmalade...

This one catches loads of people out every year. '<u>Mermelada</u>' just means <u>jam</u> — marmalade would be '<u>mermelada de naranja</u>' — '<u>orange jam</u>'. Weird but true. Now that's sorted out, <u>turn over</u>...

Food and Drink

Use '<u>me gusta</u>' and '<u>no me gusta</u>' to say what you like or don't like. Great if you're a <u>fussy eater</u>...

I like... — Me gusta / Me gustan...

Here's how to say you <u>like</u> or <u>don't like</u> something.

Remember to include 'el', 'la', 'los' or 'las' when you're saying which food and drink you like or dislike.

> <u>Me gusta</u> la nata.
> I like cream.

To like or dislike a <u>singular</u> thing, use 'me <u>gusta</u>'.

> No <u>me gusta</u> el café.
> I don't like coffee.

For more <u>foods</u>, see p.28-29.

> <u>Me gustan</u> los plátanos.
> I like bananas.

To like or dislike a <u>plural word</u> use 'me <u>gustan</u>'.

> No <u>me gustan</u> las judías.
> I don't like beans.

For more <u>opinions</u>, see p.53.

And another bit of handy <u>food vocab</u>:   Soy vegetariano/a.   I'm vegetarian.

Don't <u>say you are hungry, say you</u> <u>have hunger</u>

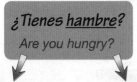

> ¿Tienes <u>hambre</u>?
> Are you hungry?

> ¿Tienes <u>sed</u>?
> Are you thirsty?

> Sí, tengo <u>hambre</u>.
> Yes, I'm hungry.

> No, gracias, no tengo <u>hambre</u>.
> No thanks, I'm not hungry.

> Sí, tengo <u>sed</u>.
> Yes, I'm thirsty.

> No, gracias, no tengo <u>sed</u>.
> No thanks, I'm not thirsty.

Mealtimes — <u>Breakfast, Lunch</u> and <u>Dinner</u>

el desayuno
breakfast

el almuerzo
lunch

la cena
dinner*

Use '<u>como</u>' (I eat) and '<u>bebo</u>' (I drink) to talk about mealtimes:

> <u>Desayuno</u> a las ocho. <u>Como</u> cereales y <u>bebo</u> un té.
> <u>I have breakfast</u> at 8 o'clock. <u>I eat</u> cereal and <u>I drink</u> tea.

> <u>Almuerzo</u> a la una. <u>Como</u> un bocadillo de queso y <u>bebo</u> un jugo.
> <u>I have lunch</u> at 1 o'clock. <u>I eat</u> a cheese sandwich and <u>I drink</u> juice.

> <u>Ceno</u> a las siete. <u>Como</u> pasta y <u>bebo</u> agua mineral.
> <u>I have dinner</u> at 7 o'clock. <u>I eat</u> pasta and <u>I drink</u> mineral water.

What's the Spanish for 'I eat all the time'...

*'<u>Dinner</u>' — also known as '<u>tea</u>' or '<u>supper</u>', depending on where you're from in the UK. Whatever you call it, it's the <u>meal</u> that's eaten in the <u>evening</u>. And you thought Spanish was <u>complicated</u>...

Food and Drink

If you go out for a <u>meal</u> in Spain, you're going to need these words...

In the restaurant — *En el restaurante*

The sign of a <u>good</u> Spanish restaurant is a paella <u>as big as the table</u>...

la camarera — *waitress*

la cuenta — *bill*

la carta — *menu*

el camarero — *waiter*

I thought you said 'camera'...

starter ➤ *el primer plato/ la entrada*
***
main course ➤ *el plato principal*
***
dessert ➤ *el postre*

Restaurant Conversations

You need to be able to ask for a <u>table</u>, order <u>food</u> and ask for the <u>bill</u>, all in <u>Spanish</u>. It's not <u>rocket science</u>, but you might go hungry if you can't do it.

1 ASKING FOR A TABLE

Replace with any number, see p.1.

Una mesa para dos, por favor. = A table for two, please.

2 ORDERING FOOD

Replace with any food or drink, see p.28-29

¿Qué quiere tomar?
= What would you like to order?

Quisiera el filete, por favor.
= I'd like steak, please.

This is a <u>formal situation</u> so the <u>waiter</u> uses '<u>quiere</u>' instead of 'quieres' and <u>you</u> use '<u>quisiera</u>' instead of 'quiero'. For more on being polite, go to <u>p.7</u>.

¿Y para beber?
= Anything to drink?

Una limonada, por favor.
= Lemonade, please.

3 PAYING

La cuenta, por favor. = The bill, please.

"Waiter, my soup tastes funny" — "So why aren't you laughing?"

One of the <u>best restaurants in the world</u> was in <u>Spain</u>, but I think it's closed now. Trouble was, you needed to be <u>super-rich</u> to eat there and you had to book <u>years in advance</u>. It's <u>only food</u>...

Clothes and Colours

Clothes — yay, let's go shopping for nice stuff. Or maybe just talk about school uniform — yawn.

Clothes — La ropa

un abrigo *coat*	una camisa *shirt*	un jersey *jumper*	un vestido *dress*	una camiseta *T-shirt*	una chaqueta *jacket*

una falda *skirt*	unos vaqueros *jeans*	unos pantalones *trousers*	unos calcetines *socks*	unos zapatos *shoes*	una corbata *tie*

unos guantes *gloves*	un sombrero *hat*

Say what you wear:

"Llevo" + "un/una/unos/unas" + ITEM OF CLOTHING

Llevo un abrigo. I wear a coat.

Some colours...

I've heard pink trainers are in fashion... Learn how to say what colour your clothes are.

negro/a	blanco/a	rojo/a	amarillo/a	azul	marrón	verde	gris	naranja	rosa
black	white	red	yellow	blue	brown	green	grey	orange	pink

Colours ending in 'o/a' change for masculine and feminine words. All the colours here change in the plural form — apart from 'naranja' and 'rosa' which never change.

The colour goes after the clothes word. It agrees with the thing it describes.

ends in 'o'
un vestido rojo   a red dress
masculine

ends in 'a'
una falda negra   a black skirt
feminine

ends in 's'
unos zapatos verdes   some green shoes
plural

Talk about your school uniform.

EL UNIFORME — UNIFORM

Llevo una corbata negra, una camisa blanca, un jersey verde y unos pantalones grises.

I wear a black tie, a white shirt, a green jumper and grey trousers.

You're so lazy you didn't even draw my hands... honestly!

Never mind that — what have you done with my head?

I can see a rainbow...

These are just some basic colours and clothes to get you started. If you want a colour that's not on this page, you can just look it up in a dictionary or on the Internet. It's as simple as that...

Clothes and Colours

You've seen the clothes, and now it's time to <u>buy them</u>. Learn how to say <u>what you want</u>.

Quisiera... — I'd like...

To buy or not to buy — that is the question... and here are the <u>answers</u>...

1

Quisiera un jersey rojo.   I'd like a red jumper.

OR

Add 'por favor' at the end to make these more polite.

¿Tiene un jersey rojo?   Do you have a red jumper?

These are both formal ways of saying what you want. See p.7 for more.

2

¿Algo más?   Anything else?

✓ *Sí, por favor.* Yes, please. OR ✗ *No, gracias.*   No thanks.

3

✓ *Lo/La compro.*   I'll buy it. OR ✗ *No lo/la compro.*   I won't buy it.

Use 'lo' if the thing you're buying is a masculine thing and 'la' if it's feminine. See p.57 for more.

"I'll buy it!"

4

And here's how to ask <u>how much things cost</u>:

¿Cuánto cuesta?   How much is it?

Cuesta veintiocho euros.   It's twenty-eight euros.

Spanish money is in Euros

Spanish money's easy. There are <u>100 cents</u> in a euro, like there are <u>100</u> pence in a pound.

This is what you'd <u>see</u> on a Spanish <u>price tag</u>: → €5,50

For numbers, see p.1.

This is how you <u>say</u> the price: → *Cinco euros con cincuenta (céntimos)* 5 euros, 50 (cents)

Money money money — essential stuff...

So maybe this page is a bit unrealistic — you'd probably just go into a <u>giant clothes store</u> and pick out the clothes without asking. But you can <u>use these phrases to buy anything</u>, not just clothes.

Summary Questions

Another set of questions to answer — lucky you. There's a lot of vocab to learn in this section so take your time, go through the questions slowly and make sure you look up any answers you get wrong. Have fun but don't get too distracted by thoughts of tasty food... Hmm pickled herrings... yum.

1) Write down two ways of asking someone how to get to the bank in Spanish.

2) What do these mean in English? a) gire a la izquierda   b) tome la primera calle a la derecha

3) Translate this conversation into Spanish.
   Helen: "Where is the market?"
   Simon: "Turn right, go straight on, take the second street on the left."
   Helen: "Is it far from here?"
   Simon: "It's two kilometres from here."

4) Write down the names of these places in Spanish: (Don't forget the 'el and 'la' bits.)
   a) butcher's   b) cake shop   c) newsagent   d) library   e) sweet shop   f) grocer's

5) What is the English for these shops?
   a) la panadería   b) el supermercado   c) el mercado   d) el banco   e) la farmacia

6) What are these places called in English?
   a) la estación   b) la iglesia   c) el museo   d) la piscina   e) la oficina de turismo

7) Write these places down in Spanish:
   a) post office   b) cinema   c) castle   d) town hall   e) leisure centre   f) theatre

8) What are these foods in Spanish?
   a)   b)   c)   d)   e)   f)   g)   h)

9) Choose four of your favourite (or least favourite) vegetables and write them down in Spanish.

10) How would you say these in Spanish?
    a) pork   b) lamb   c) beef   d) chicken   e) ham   f) sausage   g) fish

11) How do you say this list of sweet things: *cake, chocolate, biscuit, sugar, ice-cream, jam*

12) Write these drinks down in Spanish: *tea, coffee, hot chocolate, lemonade, orange juice, beer*

13) How do you say these carbs in Spanish? a) cereal b) chips c) rice d) pasta e) bread

14) In Spanish, write four sentences about what foods you like and four about foods you don't like.

15) Juan asks you "¿Tienes hambre?". How would you answer? Ask him if he's thirsty.

16) Write down what and when you usually eat for breakfast, lunch and dinner. In Spanish.

17) Write these words in Spanish:
    a) bill   b) waitress   c) waiter   d) restaurant   e) menu   f) main course

18) Write this conversation out in Spanish:
    Ana: "A table for five, please." Waiter: "What would you like?" Ana: "I'd like the pasta, please."

19) Say what you're wearing by completing this sentence: "Llevo..." Say what colour everything is.

20) Write this final conversation out in Spanish: *Ed: "Do you have a green hat?"* — Shop assistant: "Yes, anything else?" — *Ed: "No, I'll buy it."*

Sports and Musical Instruments

Those pesky Spanish teachers always ask you about <u>sports and hobbies</u>.
Learn how to say which <u>sports</u> and <u>musical instruments</u> you play.

Sports — Los deportes

Here are a few <u>popular</u> sports to get you started.

Yep, chess is technically a recognised sport...

el hockey	el fútbol	el tenis	el rugby	el ajedrez
hockey	*football*	*tennis*	*rugby*	*chess*

el baloncesto
basketball

el tenis de mesa / el ping-pong
table tennis

'al' = 'a + el' (see p.56)
If you had a '<u>la</u>' sport, you
would say 'juego <u>a la</u>...'

"Juego" + "al" + SPORT

Juego al fútbol.
I play football.

Instruments — Los instrumentos

Right, that's <u>sport</u> out of the way. Time for some <u>culture</u>...

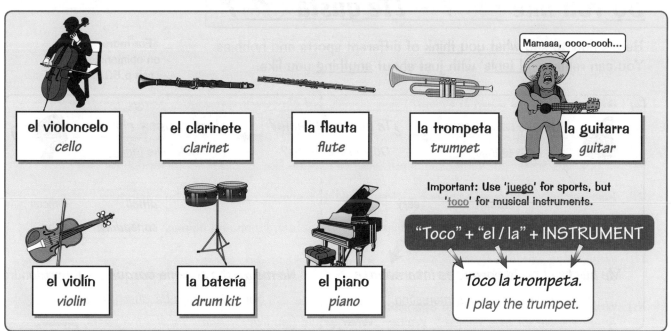

Mamaaa, oooo-oooh...

el violoncelo	el clarinete	la flauta	la trompeta	la guitarra
cello	*clarinet*	*flute*	*trumpet*	*guitar*

el violín	la batería	el piano
violin	*drum kit*	*piano*

Important: Use '<u>juego</u>' for sports, but
'<u>toco</u>' for musical instruments.

"Toco" + "el / la" + INSTRUMENT

Toco la trompeta.
I play the trumpet.

Learning these might send you instru-mental...

The catch here is using the right verb for '<u>play</u>'. Remember it's '<u>juego</u>' for <u>sports</u> and '<u>toco</u>' for <u>musical instruments</u>. Unless your band is very original and you really do use a football as a drum...

Pastimes and Hobbies

That's sport and music covered. Now let's move onto some <u>other things</u> you do in your free time.

Learn these <u>things</u> to do <u>in your</u> free time

If you have a really <u>strange</u> hobby, like <u>noodling</u>, then you're gonna need a <u>dictionary</u>...

HAGO

Hago ciclismo. *I go cycling.*

Hago esquí. *I go skiing.*

Hago aerobic. *I do aerobics.*

Hago senderismo. *I go hiking.*

Hago footing. *I go jogging.*

VOY

Voy de compras. *I go shopping.*

Voy a nadar. *I go swimming.*

*"Voy de compras" is shopping for fun — not like "Hago la compra"
on p.15 which is grocery shopping.*

Do you like 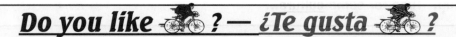 ? — ¿Te gusta ?

Here's how to say <u>what you think</u> of different sports and hobbies.
You can replace '<u>el tenis</u>' with just about <u>anything</u> you like.

*For more
on opinions,
see p.53.*

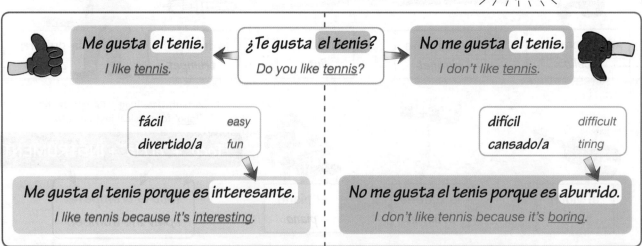

Me gusta el tenis.
I like <u>tennis</u>.

¿Te gusta el tenis?
Do you like <u>tennis</u>?

No me gusta el tenis.
I don't like <u>tennis</u>.

fácil	easy
divertido/a	fun

difícil	difficult
cansado/a	tiring

Me gusta el tenis porque es interesante.
I like tennis because it's <u>interesting</u>.

No me gusta el tenis porque es aburrido.
I don't like tennis because it's <u>boring</u>.

I've got no free time — I'm too busy learning Spanish...

Remember — "<u>I like</u>" is "<u>Me gusta</u>" + your sport or hobby. If you can give a reason why you like
it, use "<u>porque es...</u>" — "<u>because it's...</u>". Practise it with <u>loads of different words</u> until it's right.

TV, Books and Radio

I pretend I'm sporty, but really I'm on the sofa wearing a <u>sleeved blanket</u> and watching Dr Who...

I watch television — *Veo la televisión*

| Veo | la televisión. | *I watch TV.* |

Me gusta ver   I like to watch
No me gusta ver   I don't like to watch

películas   films

If you need to say '<u>the</u> film', it's '<u>la</u> película'.

I listen to music — *Escucho música*

| Escucho | música. | *I listen to music.* |

Me gusta escuchar   I like to listen to
No me gusta escuchar   I don't like to listen to

la radio   the radio

I read books — *Leo libros*

If you need to say '<u>the</u> books' etc, the articles are: '<u>los</u> libros', '<u>las</u> revistas', '<u>los</u> periódicos', '<u>las</u> novelas'.

| Leo | libros. | *I read books.* |

Me gusta leer   I like to read
No me gusta leer   I don't like to read

revistas   magazines
periódicos   newspapers
novelas   novels

I like this film — *Me gusta esta película*

You can also give your <u>opinion</u> on something <u>you've seen</u> or <u>read</u>:

That's it! I can't work with you clowns!

Me gusta...	esta película.	this film.
I like...	esta música.	this music.
No me gusta...	este libro.	this book.
I don't like...	este periódico.	this newspaper.

See p.60 for more on 'esta' and 'este'.

Books — pah! They're a thing of the past...

So now you're <u>sorted</u>. You can say what <u>hobbies</u> you have and if you like a film or not.
You're only one step away from becoming a <u>film critic</u> for a Spanish national newspaper, I reckon.

Going Out and Making Arrangements

The next two pages give you a step-by-step guide to planning a trip out.

Step 1 — Places to go

Pick your dream destination. Well, within reason...

el parque
the park

el restaurante
the restaurant

la piscina
the swimming pool

mi / tu casa
my / your house

el cine
the cinema

el centro
the town centre

el teatro
the theatre

el polideportivo
the leisure centre

Step 2 — Let's go to...

Suggest a trip out. Or learn what to say if someone asks you out (oo-er).

Use this to say, "Let's go to..."

"Vamos" + "al / a la" + PLACE

Use 'al' for 'el' words, and 'a la' for 'la' words. See p.56 for more.

Vamos a la piscina.
Let's go to the swimming pool.

Except for:

Vamos a mi casa	*Let's go to my house.*
Vamos a tu casa	*Let's go to your house.*

You don't need 'al' or 'a la' with 'mi' or 'tu'. See p.60 for more on 'my', 'your' etc.

'YES' PHRASES

Sí, por supuesto.	*Yes, of course.*
Buena idea.	*Good idea.*
¡Estupendo!	*Great!*

It's always good to give a reason if you say no.

'NO' PHRASES

No gracias.	*No, thank you.*
No me gusta la piscina.	*I don't like the swimming pool.*
No tengo dinero.	*I don't have any money.*

See p.67 for more on negative sentences.

Never turn down an invitation...

Always suggest places to go before anyone else has a chance to. Then you avoid having to go to boring places suggested by someone else. People might say you're bossy, but really, who cares?

Going Out and Making Arrangements

Step 3 — Say where and when to meet...

You know where you're <u>going</u>, so just arrange somewhere sensible to <u>meet up</u>:

Where shall we meet? — ¿Dónde nos encontramos?

Nos encontramos... *Let's meet...*	en el restaurante.	at the restaurant.
	en la piscina.	at the swimming pool.
	en tu casa.	at your house.
	delante del cine.	in front of the cinema.

What time shall we meet? — ¿Cuándo nos encontramos?

Pick a <u>specific time</u>. See pages 2-3.

> **Nos encontramos a las ocho.**   *Let's meet <u>at eight o'clock</u>.*

Or use a <u>more general</u> time phrase.

Nos encontramos... *Let's meet...*	esta noche.	tonight.
	mañana.	tomorrow.
	el lunes.	on Monday.

> Looks like I've been stood up again...

Step 4 — Buying tickets

Not much is <u>free</u> these days, so you'll probably need to <u>buy a ticket</u>:

> **¿Cuánto cuesta una entrada?**   *How much does a ticket cost?*

> **Una entrada cuesta cuatro euros.**   *A ticket costs four euros.*

> **Quisiera una entrada, por favor.**   *I'd like one ticket, please.*

You can change the <u>number of tickets</u> by changing the <u>number</u> then adding an '<u>s</u>' on the end of '<u>entrada</u>'.

I'm the one with the pink carnation...

I like to think of this page as the <u>dating page</u>. It's rather sweet, really. Although I don't think meeting in front of the <u>town hall</u> is the best start to a romantic evening, frankly, but suit yourself.

Transport P40

It's time to get from <u>A to B</u>. Pick your favourite <u>form of transport</u> here.

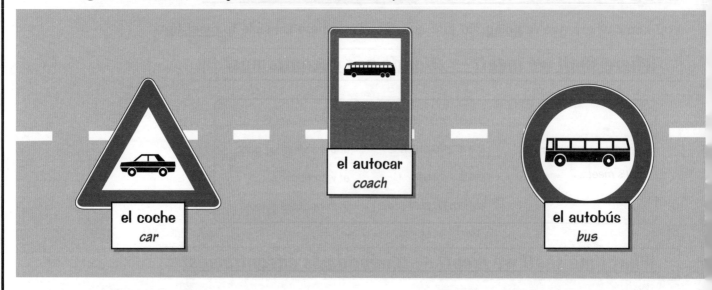

el coche
car

el autocar
coach

el autobús
bus

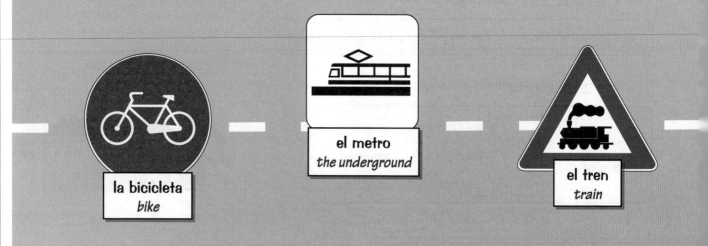

la bicicleta
bike

el metro
the underground

el tren
train

el avión
plane

la motocicleta
motorbike

el barco
boat

Let's go on a road trip...

"<u>How do you get to school?</u>" is a question you're likely to hear for <u>KS3 Spanish</u> — though you'll hear it in Spanish, obviously. Be prepared and <u>have your answer</u> ready. "By parachute", I'd say.*

Transport

Transport. Ah, the joys of the open road — the traffic jams, the fumes, the overpriced service stations...

I go by — Voy en...

Use this simple formula to say how you get places:

"Voy" + "en" + VEHICLE

Voy en...	autobús.	bus.
I go by...	tren.	train.
	coche.	car.

Of course, there's one exception:

Voy a pie.   I go on foot.

Buy tickets for travel...

Roll up, roll up, get yer transport tickets 'ere, finest Spanish vocab in taaahn.

1 ¿Hay un tren para Madrid?   *Is there a train to Madrid?*

Or 'un autocar' or 'un autobús'...

Next year we're booking a seat...

2 ¿Cuándo sale el tren para Madrid?   ¿Cuándo llega el tren a Madrid?
When does the train to Madrid leave?   *When does the train arrive in Madrid?*

El tren para Madrid sale / llega a las diez.   *The train to Madrid leaves / arrives at ten o'clock.*

3 ¿De qué andén sale el tren?   →   El tren sale del andén número dos.
Which platform does the train leave from?   *The train leaves from platform two.*

See p.2 for more times.

4 TYPES OF TICKET

| Quisiera... | un billete de ida / un billete sencillo | un billete de ida y vuelta | de primera clase | de segunda clase |
| *I would like...* | *a single ticket* | *a return ticket* | *first class* | *second class* |

EXAMPLE

Quisiera un billete de ida, de segunda clase para Madrid, por favor.
I would like a single ticket, second class to Madrid please.

A first class ticket to the Bahamas, please — one way...

Transport is worth learning about for two reasons. Firstly, it often crops up in tests. Secondly, you won't get far on your holidays if you can't even buy yourself a bus ticket and ask when it leaves.

42

Summary Questions

Yup, this section covers a fair few different things: from cricket to train tickets, from clarinets to swimming pools. Now it's time to test if all that info has sunk in. And if it hasn't — well, you know the drill. Go back over it and do the questions again until you get them 100% right.

1) Write the names of these sports in Spanish:
   a) basketball   b) table tennis   c) football   d) tennis

2) Write these sentences out in Spanish:
   a) "I play the cello."   b) "I play chess."   c) "I play the drums."

3) How do you say these things in Spanish?
   a) I go jogging.   b) I go hiking.   c) I go shopping.   d) I go cycling.

4) Answer this question in Spanish and give a reason for your answer: "¿Te gusta el hockey?"

5) What does "Me gusta ver películas" mean in English?

6) Write down what these mean in English:
   a) las revistas   b) los libros   c) las novelas   d) los periódicos

7) How would you say these phrases in Spanish?   a) "I like this film."   b) "I like this music."

8) Write the names of these places in Spanish:
   a) the park   b) the swimming pool   c) the leisure centre   d) my house

9) You're with your Spanish friend Lucas. Say "Let's go to the theatre."

10) Lucas says, "Sí, por supuesto." What does that mean in English?

11) In Spanish, tell Lucas you'll meet in front of the theatre at half past eight.

12) You and Lucas are at the theatre. How do you ask how much a ticket costs?

13) Write what these words are in Spanish:
    a) bike   b) boat   c) the underground   d) plane   e) coach

14) In Spanish, how do you say: a) I go on foot   b) I go by car   c) I go by bus

15) You're at the bus station in Valencia.
    a) How do you ask if there's a bus to Benidorm?
    b) How do you ask what time the bus to Benidorm leaves?
    c) How do you ask what time the bus arrives in Benidorm?

16) You decide you want a return train ticket to Benidorm, first class.
    How do you ask for this in Spanish?

17) You decide you've had enough of all these questions. How do you say this in Spanish?*

*I don't think we've covered this. You'd say: "Estoy harto/a de tantas preguntas."

Section 5 — Free Time, Hobbies and Transport

Post Office and Telephones

Getting postcards is great — you can learn how to send them with the useful vocab on this page. And because it's the 21st century, there's also some stuff about using the telephone.

At the post office — En la oficina de Correos

Learn the vocab below and then learn some practical sentences which use it.

un sello
a stamp

un buzón
a postbox

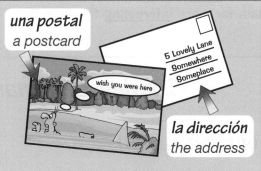

una postal
a postcard

la dirección
the address

un sobre
an envelope

una carta
a letter

> *Quisiera mandar una carta a <u>Inglaterra</u>. ¿Cuánto cuesta?*
> I would like to send a letter to <u>England</u>. How much is that?

> *Quisiera un sello para <u>Inglaterra</u> por favor.*
> I would like a stamp for <u>England</u>, please.

Change 'Inglaterra' to any country you need. See p.50 for country names.

Telephone numbers — Los números de teléfono

Being able to use the phone is practically a survival skill, so it's worth learning this well.

el número de teléfono   telephone number

Mi número de teléfono es *el cuarenta y nueve, sesenta, veintitrés.*
My telephone number is 496023.

Phone numbers in Spanish are quirky in two ways. Firstly, you introduce the number as 'el'. Secondly, you say the number in groups of two. i.e. <u>twenty-eight</u> rather than <u>two, eight</u>. See p.1 for more on numbers.

This is how you <u>answer</u> the phone:
¡Dígame!   Hello?

This is how to say <u>who you are</u>:
Hola, soy Tamara.   Hello, it's Tamara.

And this is how to ask to <u>speak to someone</u>:
¿Puedo hablar con Marco?   Can I speak to Marco?

Tony? They delivered the paella but there's somethin' fishy about it...

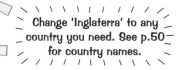

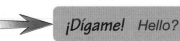

Send postcards from Spain — just to make people jealous...

And do memorise your phone number in Spanish. You never know when it'll help in an emergency...

Informal Letters

Informal letters are to people you <u>already know</u> well, or people the <u>same age as you</u>. For example, <u>postcards</u>, friendly <u>e-mails</u>, or messages on <u>social network pages</u>.

Start a letter with "Querido/a" — "Dear..."

This is a really <u>basic</u> layout for a <u>letter</u>. When you know all the other stuff in this book, you'll be able to write one with far more <u>interesting</u> things in it...

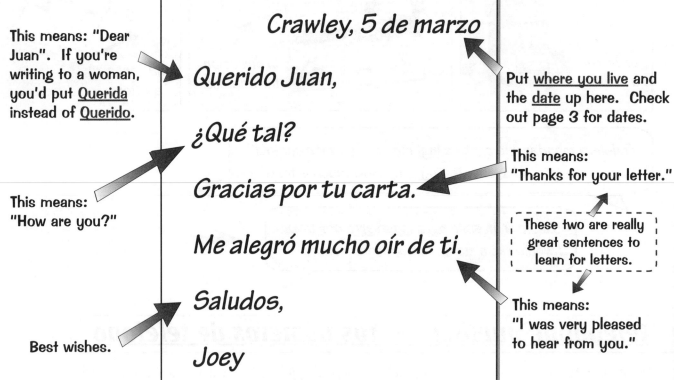

This means: "Dear Juan". If you're writing to a woman, you'd put <u>Querida</u> instead of <u>Querido</u>.

Crawley, 5 de marzo

Querido Juan,

Put <u>where you live</u> and the <u>date</u> up here. Check out page 3 for dates.

¿Qué tal?

This means: "How are you?"

Gracias por tu carta.

This means: "Thanks for your letter."

Me alegró mucho oír de ti.

These two are really great sentences to learn for letters.

Saludos,

Joey

Best wishes.

This means: "I was very pleased to hear from you."

'Sup bruvva. Woz gr8 2 get ur letter...

Other phrases to use in letters

Variety is the <u>spice of life</u>, after all.

These are all great to put at the <u>end</u> of <u>informal</u> letters, postcards and e-mails. You can use them <u>instead of</u> 'saludos'.

Escríbeme pronto.   Write soon.

Un abrazo.   A hug.

This is for people you know really well.

Hasta pronto.   Bye for now.

I reply to all my fan mail — especially if it's written in Spanish...

These phrases could come in useful in <u>lots of situations</u> — so make sure you know them <u>really well</u>. Just double check you use '<u>querido</u>' for a boy and '<u>querida</u>' for a girl when you're writing letters.

Formal Letters and Summary Questions

In <u>formal</u> situations, you need to use the right kind of <u>language</u>. You wouldn't give the manager of a travel agency 'un abrazo' and say 'hasta pronto'. Or at least, <u>you probably shouldn't</u>...

Learn the <u>set phrases</u> <u>for</u> <u>formal letters</u>

Formal letters include things like booking <u>hotel</u> rooms (see p.49) or writing to <u>companies</u>.
This is an example of a letter to <u>reserve</u> a room. You'd use the <u>same language</u> in a <u>formal e-mail</u>.

If you <u>don't</u> know the person's name, start the letter with '<u>Muy señor mío</u>' or '<u>Muy señora mía</u>'.
If you <u>do</u> know, put: '<u>Estimado</u>' to a man or '<u>Estimada</u>' to a woman. e.g.
Estimado señor García
Estimada señora Panza

Put <u>your name</u>, <u>address</u> and the <u>date</u> up here.

Chris Spackett
Salters Street
Vinegarshire
2 de junio, 2013

Muy señor mío:

Quisiera reservar una habitación doble desde el veinticinco de julio hasta el cuatro de agosto. ¿Cuánto cuesta?

This lot means:
"I'd like to reserve a double room from the 25th July to the 4th August. How much is that?"

This means:
"Yours faithfully"
or "Yours sincerely".

Le saluda atentamente,

Chris Spackett

I'm a whizz at this formal letter writing...

Just because this was a short section, it doesn't mean it was less important, or that there's not a bundle of questions for you at the end. Cover the info on the pages and have a go at these. And yes — make sure you repeat them until you get all the answers right...

1) How would you ask for an envelope in Spanish?

2) What's the Spanish word for "address"?

3) How would you give your phone number in Spanish? Use the right format.

4) List three phrases you could use at the end of an informal letter in Spanish.

5) How would you begin a formal letter in Spanish to:
    a) a woman whose name you <u>don't</u> know   b) a woman whose name you <u>do</u> know

6) How would you write "yours faithfully" in Spanish?

Weather and Seasons

You might think that because there's only <u>one type</u> of <u>weather</u> in the UK (<u>rain</u>), you'll only need to learn 'it rains'. You're wrong — teachers like to ask <u>questions</u> about <u>all types of weather</u>...

What's the weather like? — ¿Qué tiempo hace?

Make sure you learn whether each type of weather starts with '<u>hace</u>', '<u>está</u>' or '<u>hay</u>'.

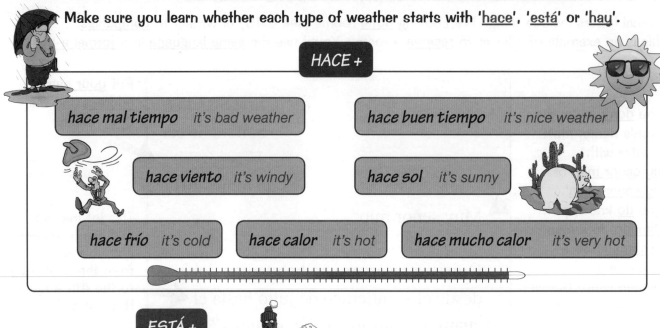

HACE +

hace mal tiempo it's bad weather	*hace buen tiempo* it's nice weather
hace viento it's windy	*hace sol* it's sunny
hace frío it's cold *hace calor* it's hot	*hace mucho calor* it's very hot

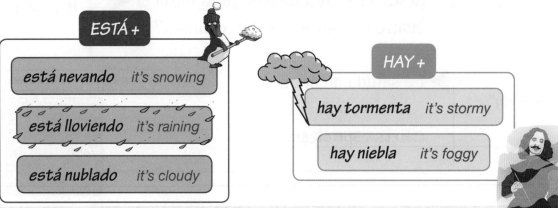

ESTÁ +

está nevando it's snowing

está lloviendo it's raining

está nublado it's cloudy

HAY +

hay tormenta it's stormy

hay niebla it's foggy

The seasons — Las estaciones

There are only <u>four seasons</u>, so you only need to learn four. <u>Brilliant</u>.

la primavera spring   *el verano* summer   *el otoño* autumn   *el invierno* winter

Siempre hace buen tiempo — not where I live...

Everyone in Britain <u>loves talking about the weather</u>, so this page has been made so you can even talk about it <u>in Spanish</u>. Practise saying what the weather's like <u>every day</u> to <u>anyone</u> who will listen.

Holidays

Teachers are <u>nosy creatures</u>. They <u>always</u> want to know <u>what you do on holiday</u>.
So, get this page learnt to be in with a <u>chance</u> of fending off their questions.

Talk about where you normally go on holiday

<u>Questions</u> are in <u>green</u>, <u>answers</u> are in <u>blue</u>, <u>underlined</u> bits are things you can <u>change</u>. Let's do this.

¿Adónde vas de vacaciones normalmente?
Where do you normally go on holiday?

¿Con quién vas de vacaciones?
Who do you go on holiday with?

Normalmente voy a <u>España</u>.
I normally go to <u>Spain</u>.

For more countries,
see <u>p.50</u>.

Voy con <u>mi padre y mi hermano</u>.
I go with <u>my dad and brother</u>.

For different people,
see <u>p.10</u>.

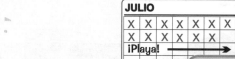

JULIO

X	X	X	X	X	X	X
X	X	X	X	X	X	
¡Playa!	→					→

| → | | | | | | |

¿Dónde te quedas?
Where do you stay?

¿Cuánto tiempo pasas allí?
How long do you spend there?

Me quedo en <u>un hotel</u>.
I stay in <u>a hotel</u>.

Go to <u>p.48</u> for
more places to stay.

Paso <u>una semana</u> allí.
I spend <u>one week</u> there.

Go to <u>p.2-3</u> for
more times.

¿Qué tiempo hace?
What is the weather like?

¿Qué haces allí?
What do you do there?

<u>Hace sol y mucho calor</u>.
<u>It's sunny and very hot</u>.

For more types of
weather, see <u>p.46</u>.

<u>Voy a la playa</u>.
<u>I go to the beach</u>.

For more things to do,
see <u>p.35-38</u>.

This is worse than the Spanish Inquisition...

Phew — there are loads of questions here. <u>Learn the question</u> that goes with each <u>answer</u> so that
when your teacher starts <u>firing questions at you</u>, you know what they're <u>asking</u>. Go, go, go...

Hotels and Camping

Here's everything you need to know about going on holiday to a Spanish-speaking country. It's also pretty handy in class when you're talking about where you normally go on holiday. Enjoy.

Some places to stay

Here are some places you might stay in.

el hotel	*hotel*

el albergue juvenil	*youth hostel*

el camping	*campsite*

At the campsite — En el camping

Learn this important camping vocabulary.

la tienda	*tent*

el saco de dormir	*sleeping bag*

la caravana	*caravan*

la parcela	*pitch*

el agua potable	*drinking water*

At the hotel — En el hotel

Some more really useful hotel vocabulary for you.

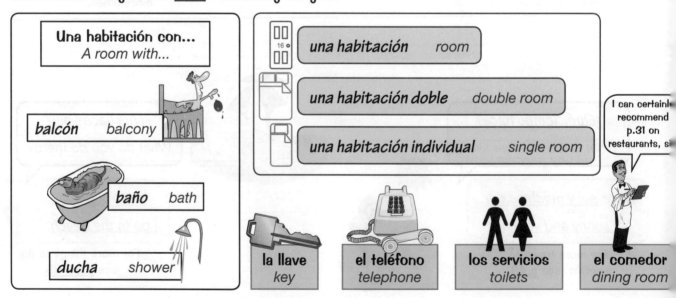

Una habitación con...
A room with...

balcón balcony

baño bath

ducha shower

una habitación	room
una habitación doble	double room
una habitación individual	single room

I can certainl[y] recommend p.31 on restaurants, s[o]

la llave	*key*

el teléfono	*telephone*

los servicios	*toilets*

el comedor	*dining room*

Call me a princess, but I don't do camping...

There's loads of vocab on this page, but it's dead important for being able to talk about holidays. Cover the page, scribble down what you remember and check it. Try again if something's not right.

Booking Accommodation

Being able to book a holiday is pretty <u>clever</u> stuff. This page has got all the <u>questions and answers</u> you'll need — there's <u>a lot</u> of stuff to learn here so <u>take your time</u>.

Booking a hotel room — tell them what and when

Learning how to <u>book a hotel room</u> is really useful, not just in class but in <u>real life</u> too.
The <u>questions</u> in <u>blue</u> are the ones that the <u>receptionist</u> will ask <u>you</u>.

The questions here are in the <u>polite form</u>. To learn more about how to be polite, go to <u>p.7</u>.

1 ¿Tiene una habitación libre?   Do you have any free rooms?

2 ¿Qué tipo de habitación quiere?

Quisiera	una habitación individual	a single room
I would like	una habitación doble	a double room

Quisiera una habitación individual.
Quisiera quedarme dos noches desde el siete de mayo hasta el nueve de mayo. ¿Cuánto cuesta?

3 ¿Cuántas noches quiere quedarse?

Quisiera quedarme	una noche	one night
I would like to stay	dos semanas	two weeks

For other numbers, see <u>p.1</u>.

Cuesta €150.

4 ¿Cuándo quiere quedarse?

Quisiera quedarme desde	el cinco de julio	hasta	el diez de julio
I would like to stay from	the fifth of July	until	the tenth of July

For other dates, see <u>p.3</u>.

5 ¿Cuánto cuesta?   How much is that?

Booking into a campsite — ask for "una parcela"

Use the <u>same phrases</u> to book into a <u>campsite</u> as you would a hotel (except the first two) — just don't forget to ask for '<u>una parcela</u>' instead of 'una habitación'.

1 ¿Tiene una parcela libre?   Do you have a free pitch?

2 ¿Qué tipo de parcela quiere?

Quisiera una parcela para	una tienda	a tent
I would like a pitch for	una caravana	a caravan

Oh jolly good. Looks spiffing — does it have a Jacuzzi bath?

"Yes I'm sure I want a pitch for a tent, not a shop..."

As you've probably guessed by now, '<u>tienda</u>' is used for both '<u>tent</u>' and '<u>shop</u>' — it's all down to the <u>context</u>. Learn this page — your teacher's bound to want you to do <u>hotel and campsite role plays</u>.

Countries

Luckily, you don't need to be good at <u>geography</u> for this page — you just need to <u>remember</u> all the <u>countries in Spanish</u>. Don't get <u>distracted</u> by all the pleasant shades of <u>green</u> though.

Countries — _Los países_

['el país' = country]

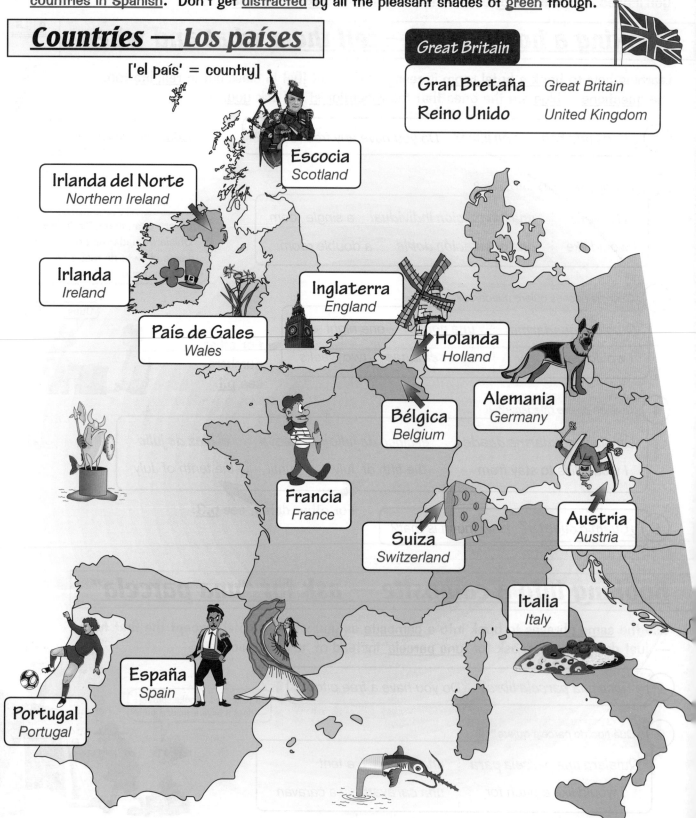

Great Britain

Gran Bretaña	_Great Britain_
Reino Unido	_United Kingdom_

Escocia
Scotland

Irlanda del Norte
Northern Ireland

Irlanda
Ireland

Inglaterra
England

País de Gales
Wales

Holanda
Holland

Alemania
Germany

Bélgica
Belgium

Francia
France

Suiza
Switzerland

Austria
Austria

Italia
Italy

España
Spain

Portugal
Portugal

No stereotypes were harmed in the making of this page...

Okay, not <u>all</u> Spanish people wear flamenco dresses, but the point of this page is to <u>learn the</u> <u>countries in Spanish</u>. <u>Look</u> at the map, <u>cover it</u> and <u>see how many countries</u> you remember.

Nationalities

People always want to know <u>where you're from</u>. In fact, I'd eat my hat if it wasn't one of the <u>first questions</u> you're asked when you meet someone new, so make sure you know how to <u>answer</u> it.

Where do you live? — ¿Dónde vives?

I live under a bridge.

Learn to say <u>where you live</u>:

> "Vivo en" + COUNTRY

Vivo en Inglaterra.
I live in England.

Vivo en País de Gales.
I live in Wales.

Vivo en Escocia.
I live in Scotland.

Vivo en Irlanda del Norte.
I live in Northern Ireland.

Talk about your nationality

This is how to say what <u>nationality</u> you are. Remember that nationality words <u>change</u> depending on whether you're <u>male</u> or <u>female</u>, and if you're <u>female</u>, you <u>don't</u> need an accent on the final '<u>e</u>'.

> You don't need a capital letter for nationalities in Spanish.

> "Soy" + NATIONALITY

Soy inglés.
Soy inglesa.
I'm English.

Soy galés.
Soy galesa.
I'm Welsh.

Soy escocés.
Soy escocesa.
I'm Scottish.

Soy norirlandés.
Soy norirlandesa.
I'm Northern Irish.

Some other nationalities

A few more <u>important nationalities</u> for you to learn. You never know when they might <u>crop up</u>...

francés
francesa
French

español
española
Spanish

alemán
alemana
German

italiano
italiana
Italian

irlandés
irlandesa
Irish

Soy inglés — that's weird, I always thought soy was Chinese...

"<u>Where do you live?</u>" is a nosy foreigner's <u>favourite question</u>, so learn how to <u>reply</u> to them.
Learn the <u>questions</u> on this page too so you can ask them <u>in return</u>. Now you're a nosy foreigner...

Summary Questions

Wow, there was a lot to get your head around in that section. So, luckily for you, here's a page of questions so you can make sure you've learnt everything. If you don't know the answers to any of the questions, flick back through the section, find the answers and do the questions again. Don't stop until you can answer every question blindfolded and standing on your head. And look on the bright side — now you'll be able to book a camping trip somewhere considerably hotter than the UK...

1) Your Spanish friend, Javier, wants to know what the weather is like in the UK. Say that it is cold and raining.

2) Javier says that it's hot and sunny. How would he say that in Spanish?

3) Write down all four seasons in Spanish.

4) You're telling Eva about where you normally go on holiday. Say this in Spanish:
*"Normally I go to Italy. I go with my mother and my sister.
I spend one week there. I stay in a hotel. I go swimming."*

5) How would you say these in Spanish? a) youth hostel   b) campsite

6) What are these in Spanish?
a) tent   b) drinking water   c) pitch   d) caravan   e) sleeping bag

7) Write these down in Spanish:
a) key   b) single room   c) double room   d) room with a bath   e) dining room

8) You walk into a hotel in Barcelona. Ask if they have any rooms free.

9) Tell them you'd like a single room with a balcony.

10) Say you want to stay for 3 nights from 5th March to 8th March. Ask how much it costs.

11) You arrive at a campsite in Peru. In Spanish, ask if they have a free pitch.

12) Tell them you'd like a pitch for a tent for two weeks.

13) Say you want to stay from the 6th September until the 13th September.

14) Write down all four countries in the UK.

15) What's the Spanish for these?
a) France   b) Holland   c) Italy   d) Ireland   e) Austria   f) Spain

16) What are these in English?
a) Suiza   b) Alemania   c) Portugal   d) Bélgica

17) Write down in Spanish where you live and your nationality.

18) Write down in Spanish the <u>nationalities</u> that go with these places:
a) France   b) Spain   c) Italy   d) Germany   e) Ireland   f) Scotland   g) Wales

Opinions

If you're learning Spanish, it's really, _really_ important to learn how to <u>give an opinion</u> and <u>back it up</u>.

Talk about your <u>likes</u> and <u>dislikes</u>

Remember to use 'el', 'la', 'los' or 'las' with 'me gusta(n)'.

'<u>Me gusta</u>' changes depending on whether the thing you like is <u>singular</u> or <u>plural</u>. Make sure you learn <u>both</u> endings and use the <u>right one</u>. Check out the examples.

Me gusta	I like (singular)
Me gustan	I like (plural)

No me gusta	I don't like (singular)
No me gustan	I don't like (plural)

Me gusta la comida.	I like food.
Me gustan los zapatos.	I like the shoes.

No me gusta el arte.	I don't like art.
No me gustan los deportes.	I don't like sports.

Here are some <u>other</u> ways of expressing your opinion:

Me gusta(n) mucho	I like ... a lot
Me encanta(n)	I love

No me gusta(n) nada	I don't like ... at all
Odio	I hate

'Me encanta' changes just like 'me gusta'.

Me encantan las matemáticas.
I love maths.

No me gusta nada estudiar.
I don't like to study at all.

Use the <u>infinitive</u> form of the verb with 'gustar' (see <u>p.62</u> for more on the infinitive).

Explain why — <u>Porque</u> = Because

Use the phrase '<u>porque es</u>' (because it is) or '<u>porque son</u>' (because they are) to <u>explain</u> an opinion. Then use these <u>describing words</u> (adjectives) to make some really impressive Spanish phrases.

THE GOOD	
bueno/a	good
estupendo/a	great
fantástico/a	fantastic
genial	brilliant

THE BAD	
horrible	awful
aburrido	boring
difícil	difficult
malo/a	bad

THE PRETTY USEFUL	
precioso/a	beautiful, lovely
fácil	easy
interesante	interesting
agradable	nice / kind
simpático/a	nice (people only)
raro/a	strange
divertido/a	fun

Here's how you <u>string it all together</u>:

verb | A noun or the infinitive here | 'porque es' = 'because it is' | Describing word

Odio | _limpiar la casa_ | _porque es_ | _aburrido._

<u>I hate</u> <u>to clean the house</u> <u>because it is</u> <u>boring.</u>

See p.58 for adjectives and agreements.

SPANISH DICTIONARY

For more describing words, consult one of these.

<u>Me encanta el español porque es fantástico...</u>

If you disagree, learn how to say otherwise. Either way, you have to learn the stuff on this page.

Asking Questions

You won't get very far in Spain if you can't ask any <u>questions</u>. That's where this page comes in.

Use ¿ and ? and your *tone of voice*

<u>Question marks</u> and <u>tone of voice</u> show that you're asking a question, even if you're not using a <u>question word</u>.

1 In Spanish, you can turn a <u>statement</u> into a <u>question</u> by using a pair of <u>question marks</u>. The upside down one goes at the <u>start</u> of the question and the normal one goes at the <u>end</u>.

2 When you're talking, make your <u>voice</u> go <u>up</u> at the end. This will show that you're asking a <u>question</u>.

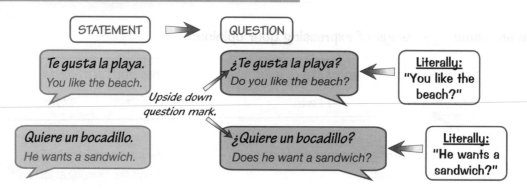

STATEMENT ⟹ QUESTION

Te gusta la playa.
You like the beach.

¿Te gusta la playa?
Do you like the beach?

Literally:
"You like the beach?"

Upside down question mark.

Quiere un bocadillo.
He wants a sandwich.

¿Quiere un bocadillo?
Does he want a sandwich?

Literally:
"He wants a sandwich?"

Use a *question word*

Ah yes, there are <u>quite a lot</u> of these. These are <u>short</u> words, but they're <u>important</u>, so you pretty much have to <u>learn them all</u> (and their <u>accents</u> too). Just remember:

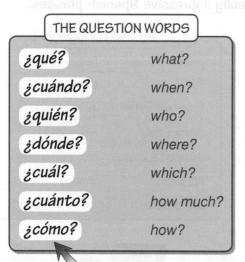

THE QUESTION WORDS	
¿qué?	what?
¿cuándo?	when?
¿quién?	who?
¿dónde?	where?
¿cuál?	which?
¿cuánto?	how much?
¿cómo?	how?

1) <u>Question words</u> usually come <u>before the verb</u> in a question.

2) You always need <u>both question marks</u>.

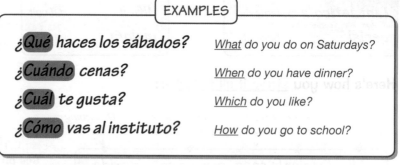

Why so many questions?

EXAMPLES	
¿Qué haces los sábados?	<u>What</u> do you do on Saturdays?
¿Cuándo cenas?	<u>When</u> do you have dinner?
¿Cuál te gusta?	<u>Which</u> do you like?
¿Cómo vas al instituto?	<u>How</u> do you go to school?

"¿Cómo?" can sometimes mean "<u>What?</u>" too. For example,
"¿Cómo te llamas?" means "<u>What</u> are you called?".

Now you're ready for a game of twenty questions in Spanish...

<u>Upside down question marks</u> might look <u>funny</u> to us, but they really are <u>necessary</u> in Spanish. Don't forget about them. The more you <u>practise using them</u>, the more <u>normal</u> they'll start to look.

Words for People and Objects

This stuff might be a bit <u>fiddly</u> at first but it's not so bad once you <u>get the hang of it</u>.

Every Spanish noun is masculine or feminine

I'd love to tell you <u>why</u> Spanish nouns are <u>masculine or feminine</u>, but it's just <u>one of those things</u>.

1) Spanish words for '<u>the</u>' and '<u>a</u>' change to match the gender (masculine or feminine) of the word. See <u>p.56</u> for more on '<u>a</u>' and '<u>the</u>'.

> MASCULINE
>
> <u>el</u> lápiz   <u>the</u> pencil
> <u>un</u> lápiz   <u>a</u> pencil

> FEMININE
>
> <u>la</u> falda   <u>the</u> skirt
> <u>una</u> falda   <u>a</u> skirt

> **THE GOLDEN RULE**
> Each time you learn a word,
> learn the 'el' or 'la' to go with
> it. Don't think 'gato = cat',
> think '<u>el</u> gato' = cat'.

2) <u>Describing words</u> (adjectives) also change to match the <u>gender</u> of the noun. So a <u>masculine noun</u> needs a <u>masculine describing word</u>. See <u>p.58</u> for more on <u>adjective endings</u>.

Making nouns plural

A <u>plural</u> noun simply means <u>more than one</u> of something. Here's how to turn <u>singular nouns</u> into <u>plural nouns</u> in Spanish.

> If the vowel before the last consonant has an accent, then the accent disappears in the plural.

1) If the noun ends in a <u>vowel</u>, you add '<u>s</u>'. If it ends in a <u>consonant</u>, you usually add '<u>es</u>'.

> una manzana   an apple
> dos manzana<u>s</u>   two apples

> un tomate   a tomato
> dos tomate<u>s</u>   two tomatoes

> un limón   a lemon
> dos limon<u>es</u>   two lemons

2) BUT, if a noun ends in '<u>z</u>', you have to change the '<u>z</u>' to a '<u>c</u>' and add '<u>es</u>'.

> un lápiz   a pencil
> dos lá<u>pices</u>   two pencils

> The <u>Golden Rule</u> works here as well.
> Each time you learn a new word,
> learn how to make it plural.

3) When you make a noun plural, you also have to change the way you say '<u>the</u>'. (See p.56.) For masculine nouns, '<u>el</u>' becomes 'los'. For feminine nouns, '<u>la</u>' becomes '<u>las</u>'.

> el lápiz   the pencil
> los lápices   the pencils

> la falda   the skirt
> las faldas   the skirts

Masculine and feminine words? Isn't that sexism or something?

Because this is so different to English, it may take a bit of <u>getting used to</u>. Just follow the advice in the <u>Golden Rule</u> box. Learn those little words <u>straight off</u> and you'll do yourself a <u>massive favour</u>.

How to say 'The' and 'A'

These words might be <u>small</u>, but you won't be getting far without them. You'll use them <u>all the time</u> so it's worth getting to grips with them <u>ASAP</u>.

> It's time to take on articles — and win!

'The' — el, la, los, las

1) The Spanish word for '<u>the</u>' changes depending on:
   - Whether a word is <u>masculine</u> or <u>feminine</u>.
   - Whether a word is <u>singular</u> or <u>plural</u>.

> Grammar Fans: these are called '<u>Definite Articles</u>'.

THE	MASCULINE	FEMININE
SINGULAR	EL	LA
PLURAL	LOS	LAS

el coche   the car   →   *los coches*   the cars

la casa   the house   →   *las casas*   the houses

One exception is '<u>el agua</u>' (water). '<u>Agua</u>' is feminine even though it goes with '<u>el</u>'.

2) You can't say '<u>a el</u>' ('<u>to the</u>') or '<u>de el</u>' ('<u>of the</u>' or '<u>from the</u>') in Spanish. Instead you say '<u>al</u>' (a + el) and '<u>del</u>' (de + el) before a <u>masculine noun</u>.

> You'd use '<u>a la</u>' and '<u>de la</u>' for feminine nouns.

'a' + 'el' = 'al'

Vamos al parque.   We go <u>to the</u> park.
Voy al camping.   I go <u>to the</u> campsite.

'de' + 'el' = 'del'

> Literally, "The book <u>of</u> the teacher."

El libro del profesor.   The teacher's book.
Soy del Reino Unido.   I'm <u>from the</u> UK.

'A' — un, una

Just like the word for '<u>the</u>', the word for '<u>a</u>' changes too.

> Grammar Fans: these are called '<u>Indefinite Articles</u>'.

1) When you make '<u>un</u>' or '<u>una</u>' plural, they mean '<u>some</u>' or '<u>a few</u>'.

A	
MASCULINE	FEMININE
UN	UNA

SOME	
MASCULINE	FEMININE
UNOS	UNAS

Tengo un caballo.   I have <u>a</u> horse.
Tengo unos caballos.   I have <u>some</u> horses.

Tengo una pera.   I have <u>a</u> pear.
Tengo unas peras.   I have <u>some</u> pears.

2) You don't always use the Spanish word for '<u>a</u>' when you would use it in English. For example, you <u>leave it out</u>:

- after the verb '<u>ser</u>' for <u>someone's occupation</u>

  Es médica.   She's a doctor.

- in <u>negative sentences</u>.

  No tengo animales en casa.
  I don't have any pets.

And notice that in Spanish, there isn't a special word for '<u>any</u>'.

Who knew such small words could be such a massive pain...

'<u>El</u>' and '<u>un</u>' are masculine, '<u>la</u>' and '<u>una</u>' are feminine. '<u>Los</u>', '<u>las</u>', '<u>unos</u>' and '<u>unas</u>' are plural. This stuff <u>can</u> be simple. <u>Do</u> learn when to <u>leave out the article</u> though — that's a common error.

I, You, Him, Them...

Pronouns are handy words which save you from repeating nouns. For example, 'he', 'she' and 'they'.

'He' is the pronoun. It means you don't have to use 'Sancho' again.

Sancho loves tacos. He eats tacos every day.

I, you, he, she — Yo, tú, él, ella

Subject pronouns (like 'I', 'he', 'they') are not as common in Spanish as they are in English. They're optional and are usually used for emphasis or to make it clear who you're talking about.

The '-as' endings are for groups of girls only.
The '-os' endings can be for boys or a mixed group.

I =	yo	nosotros/as	= we
you (singular) =	tú	vosotros/as	= you (plural)
he =	él	ellos	= they (boys + mixed)
she =	ella	ellas	= they (girls only)

Grammar Fans: these are called 'Subject Pronouns'.

Ellas compran pan.
They (the girls) buy bread.

Sara y Marta compran pan.
Sara and Marta buy bread.

Compran pan.
They buy bread.

You don't need the pronoun 'ellas' as the verb ending tells you who (or what) is doing the action, but using it makes it clearer who you're talking about.

Me, you, him — Me, te, lo

Take this sentence: 'Helen plays the guitar.' A direct object pronoun can replace 'the guitar' because it's the noun having the action done to it — 'Helen plays it.'

me =	me	nos	= us
you (singular) =	te	os	= you (plural)
him / it =	lo	los	= them (masculine)
her / it =	la	las	= them (feminine)

Grammar Fans: these are called 'Direct Object Pronouns'.

Watch it. The direct object pronoun moves in the sentence to go before the verb. Don't forget...

Paz come la tarta.
Paz eats the cake.
→ *Paz la come.*
Paz eats it.

Luis lava el perro.
Luis washes the dog.
→ *Luis lo lava.*
Luis washes it.

Pronouns — or pr-Oh No-ns if you're having a bad day...
Terrible word play, I know, but all this grammar is enough to go to anyone's head.

Words to Describe Things

Adjectives in Spanish work differently to English. They change to match the noun they go with.

Adjectives 'agree' with what they're describing

1) In English, describing words (adjectives) don't change. You can have a tall boy, tall boys, a tall girl and tall girls. The word 'tall' stays the same.

> Grammar Fans: these are called 'Adjectives'.

2) In Spanish, the describing word has to match the word it's describing — whether it's masculine or feminine, singular or plural.

3) Here's how the adjective changes to agree with different nouns. I've used 'blanco' (white) as an example.

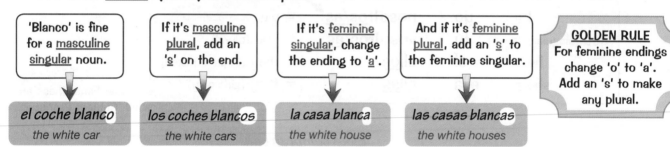

'Blanco' is fine for a masculine singular noun.	If it's masculine plural, add an 's' on the end.	If it's feminine singular, change the ending to 'a'.	And if it's feminine plural, add an 's' to the feminine singular.

GOLDEN RULE
For feminine endings change 'o' to 'a'. Add an 's' to make any plural.

el coche blanco	los coches blancos	la casa blanca	las casas blancas
the white car	the white cars	the white house	the white houses

4) If an adjective ends in '-e', it stays the same for masculine and feminine words. You just add an 's' to the adjectives when the noun is plural.

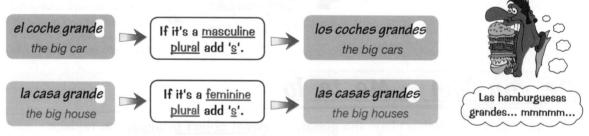

el coche grande	→	If it's a masculine plural add 's'.	→	los coches grandes
the big car				the big cars

la casa grande	→	If it's a feminine plural add 's'.	→	las casas grandes
the big house				the big houses

Las hamburguesas grandes... mmmmm...

Most describing words go after the noun

In English, the describing word goes in front of the noun. We say 'the hot soup' not 'the soup hot'. But not in Spanish...

Literally, "I want a sandwich big."

Quiero un bocadillo grande.	Tienen dos bicicletas nuevas.	"Tengo un hámster raro."
I want a big sandwich	They have two new bikes.	"I have a strange hamster."

I'm sure you can think of many words to describe this page...

...though maybe not all of them would be particularly nice. That aside though, it's really important to check your work to make sure all the nouns and describing words agree. Make it a habit.

Making Comparisons

Comparing things is pretty handy when you're describing stuff. Read this page and have a go...

'Más' is 'more' and 'menos' is 'less'

1) In Spanish you can't say 'bigger' or 'biggest'. You have to say 'more big' or 'the most big'.

'Más' means 'more'

'El más' means 'the most'

EXAMPLES

Mi sombrero es grande.	Mi sombrero es más grande.	Mi sombrero es el más grande.
My hat is big.	My hat is bigger.	My hat is the biggest.

2) To say that something is 'less' something, use the word 'menos':

EXAMPLES

'Menos' means 'less'.

'El menos' means 'the least'.

Raúl es menos perezoso.	Raúl es el menos perezoso.
Raúl is less lazy.	Raúl is the least lazy.

> **Grammar Fans:**
> 'More' and 'less' words are 'Comparatives'. 'The most' and 'the least' words are 'Superlatives'.

3) 'El más' and 'el menos' change to 'la más/la menos' if a noun is feminine singular and to 'los/las más' and 'los/las menos' for masculine and feminine plurals.

Mis gatos son los más gordos.	Esta clase es la menos aburrida.
My cats are the most fat (fattest).	This class is the least boring.

← *Remember that the describing word still has to agree with the noun (p.58)*

4) These are the odd ones out:

GOOD, BETTER, BEST		BAD, WORSE, WORST		OLD, OLDER, OLDEST		YOUNG, YOUNGER, YOUNGEST	
bueno	good	malo	bad	viejo	old	joven	young
mejor	better	peor	worse	mayor	older	menor	younger
el mejor	the best	el peor	the worst	el mayor	the oldest	el menor	the youngest

Learn these three great ways of comparing things

Use these handy phrases to compare things: 'más...que' ('more...than'), 'menos...que' ('less...than') and 'tan...como' ('as...as').

MÁS...QUE	MENOS...QUE	TAN...COMO
Soy más alto que tú.	Soy menos alto que tú.	Soy tan alto como tú.
I am taller than you.	I am less tall than you.	I am as tall as you.

"Comparison is the thief of joy..." Theodore Roosevelt

'Teddy' Roosevelt famously survived an assassination attempt in 1912. The bullet that should have killed him was stopped by his glasses case which he always carried in his top pocket. Lucky chap.

'My' and 'Your' — 'This' and 'These'

Sometimes, grammar boils down to simply learning lots of incredibly useful little words.

How to say 'my', 'your', 'our'...

Grammar Fans: these are called 'Possessive Adjectives'.

1) In English, you use words like 'my', 'your' or 'her' to show that something belongs to someone. In Spanish, these words change...

2) The table shows these words in Spanish and (you guessed it) they come in masculine, feminine, singular and plural forms.

3) Important: the possessive adjectives agree with the thing — not the person they belong to.

	masculine singular	feminine singular	masculine plural	feminine plural
my	mi	mi	mis	mis
your (singular)	tu	tu	tus	tus
his/her/its	su	su	sus	sus
our	nuestro	nuestra	nuestros	nuestras
your (plural)	vuestro	vuestra	vuestros	vuestras
their (plural)	su	su	sus	sus

Yep, that's right, 'su(s)' can mean 'his', 'her', 'its' or 'their'.

Tengo tus zapatos y tu corbata.
I have your shoes and your tie.

Mi hermano va al parque con sus amigos.
My brother goes to the park with his friends.

How to say 'this' and 'that'

Grammar Fans: these are called 'Demonstrative Adjectives'.

Oh yes. More words that have to agree with the nouns they go with.

	MASCULINE	FEMININE
THIS	este	esta
THAT	ese	esa
THESE	estos	estas
THOSE	esos	esas

EXAMPLES

Esta casa. This house.

Ese tren. That train.

Estos libros. These books.

Esas sillas. Those chairs.

Lucky you — even more examples.

Esta casa es mi casa.
This house is my house.

Ese tren es nuestro tren.
That train is our train.

A little bit of this, a little bit of that...

OK, so there's a lot of info in these tables, but don't let that put you off. Remember, you're bigger and better than them. Just practise using these words over and over until they're second nature.

'Por' and 'Para'

'Por' and 'para' confuse nearly everyone. They can both mean 'for', but in different situations.
Learn these examples and use them to help you decide when you need to use each one.

Use Para for...

1) Saying who something is for:

> *El zumo es para Paula.*   The juice is <u>for</u> Paula.

2) Talking about a destination:

> *El avión para Barcelona*   The plane <u>to</u> Barcelona

For other kinds of transport,
take a trip to p.40. See ya...

3) When you want to say 'to'/'in order to':

> *Voy al parque para jugar al fútbol.*   I go to the park <u>in order to</u> play football.

4) Specific periods of time when you're talking about the future:

> *Voy a ir a España para una semana.*   I am going to go to Spain <u>for</u> a week.

5) When you want to say 'by' in time phrases:

> *"Haga los deberes para mañana."*   "Do the homework <u>by</u> tomorrow."

See p.69 for
the imperative.

Use Por for...

Watch out: <u>after a time</u>, 'por' changes to '<u>de</u>' — e.g. 'son
las ocho <u>de</u> la mañana' (it's eight o'clock in the morning).

1) Talking about parts of the <u>day</u>:

| *por la mañana* | *por la tarde* | *por la noche* |
| in the morning | in the afternoon/evening | at night |

2) When you say 'through':

> *Voy por el mercado.*   I go <u>through</u> the market.

3) Exchanges, like prices or amounts of money:

> *Pago dos euros por el autobús.*   I pay two euros <u>for</u> the bus.

4) Saying 'thank you <u>for</u>...':

> *Gracias por las salchichas.*   Thank you <u>for</u> the sausages.

*"Dear Aunty Carol,
Thank you for the sausages..."*

Por and para — good for confusing students...

This is <u>tricky</u>, and there'll be times when you get a <u>bit confused</u> by it all. But if you can do your
best to <u>memorise</u> what kind of sentences use '<u>por</u>' or '<u>para</u>' you'll make loads fewer errors.

Verbs in the Present Tense

It's time to get <u>technical</u> and learn <u>how to deal</u> with <u>verbs</u>... Good luck.

The <u>infinitive</u> means 'to + verb'

When you look up a Spanish <u>verb</u> in a dictionary, you'll find the <u>infinitive</u>, like '<u>hablar</u>' or '<u>comer</u>'.
In Spanish, the infinitive is made of a '<u>stem</u>' and an '<u>ending</u>'.
The 'ending' is the <u>last two letters</u> of the infinitive.

This is how to form the <u>present tense</u> in Spanish:

① *Find the verb stem.*

② *Add on the new ending.*

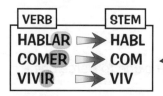

VERB		STEM
HABLAR	➡	HABL
COMER	➡	COM
VIVIR	➡	VIV

To find the <u>stem</u>, all you need to do is <u>take off</u> the <u>last two letters</u> of the <u>infinitive</u>.

These are the <u>endings</u> you need to add:

Endings for *-ar* verbs

ARRRRRRR!

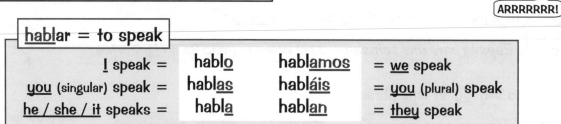

<u>hablar</u> = to speak			
<u>I</u> speak =	habl<u>o</u>	habl<u>amos</u>	= <u>we</u> speak
<u>you</u> (singular) speak =	habl<u>as</u>	habl<u>áis</u>	= <u>you</u> (plural) speak
<u>he / she / it</u> speaks =	habl<u>a</u>	habl<u>an</u>	= <u>they</u> speak

Endings for *-er* verbs

To form the <u>polite 'you'</u> (singular) for <u>any verb</u>, use the '<u>he/she/it</u>' part. For <u>polite 'you'</u> (plural) use the '<u>they</u>' part. See <u>p.7</u> for more.

<u>comer</u> = to eat			
<u>I</u> eat =	com<u>o</u>	com<u>emos</u>	= <u>we</u> eat
<u>you</u> (singular) eat =	com<u>es</u>	com<u>éis</u>	= <u>you</u> (plural) eat
<u>he / she / it</u> eats =	com<u>e</u>	com<u>en</u>	= <u>they</u> eat

Endings for *-ir* verbs

<u>vivir</u> = to live			
<u>I</u> live =	viv<u>o</u>	viv<u>imos</u>	= <u>we</u> live
<u>you</u> (singular) live =	viv<u>es</u>	viv<u>ís</u>	= <u>you</u> (plural) live
<u>he / she / it</u> lives =	viv<u>e</u>	viv<u>en</u>	= <u>they</u> live

The stem doesn't change for any regular verbs.

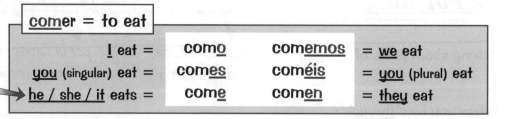

EXAMPLE	1) Start by <u>removing</u> the <u>last two</u> letters:	2) Then <u>add on</u> the new ending:	3) And <u>there you go</u>...
To say '<u>I speak</u> Spanish':	habla̶r̶	habl⟵o	*Hablo español.* = <u>I speak</u> Spanish.

Verbs in the Present Tense

A <u>few common verbs</u> follow a pattern that's a <u>bit different</u> to regular verbs...

Some Spanish verbs *change their stem*

> Grammar Fans: these are called '<u>stem-changing</u>' or '<u>radical-changing</u>' verbs.

1) Some <u>verb stems change their spelling</u> in the present tense.
2) The '<u>e</u>' in the stem changes to an '<u>ie</u>' or the '<u>o</u>' changes to a '<u>ue</u>' (remember this only applies to <u>certain verbs</u> called <u>stem-changing verbs</u>).
3) Stem-changing verbs <u>don't change</u> in the '<u>we</u>' and '<u>you</u>' (plural) forms.
4) Here are <u>three really common ones</u> that <u>do</u> change their stem:

E ➡ IE

> The <u>endings</u> are the <u>same</u> as <u>regular verbs</u>.

The first '<u>e</u>' in 'qu<u>e</u>rer' changes to '<u>ie</u>' (except for 'we' and 'you' plural).

querer = to want

<u>I</u> want =	quiero	queremos	= <u>we</u> want
<u>you</u> (singular) want =	quieres	queréis	= <u>you</u> (plural) want
<u>he / she / it</u> wants =	quiere	quieren	= <u>they</u> want

The first 'e' in 't<u>e</u>ner' also changes to '<u>ie</u>' (except for 'we' and 'you' plural). The '<u>I</u>' form of 'tener' ('<u>tengo</u>') is <u>completely irregular</u>.

tener = to have

<u>I</u> have =	tengo	tenemos	= <u>we</u> have
<u>you</u> (singular) have =	tienes	tenéis	= <u>you</u> (plural) have
<u>he / she / it</u> has =	tiene	tienen	= <u>they</u> have

O ➡ UE

The '<u>o</u>' in 'p<u>o</u>der' changes to '<u>ue</u>' (except for 'we' and 'you' plural).

o...ue...o...ue

poder = to be able to

<u>I</u> can =	puedo	podemos	= <u>we</u> can
<u>you</u> (singular) can =	puedes	podéis	= <u>you</u> (plural) can
<u>he / she / it</u> can =	puede	pueden	= <u>they</u> can

Remember: use the '<u>he/she/it</u>' part to form the polite '<u>you</u>' (<u>singular</u>) and the '<u>they</u>' part for the polite '<u>you</u>' (<u>plural</u>) of any verb.

Tener a tenner is to be rich...

The <u>stem-changing</u> verbs are a bit of a pain, but if you learn '<u>querer</u>', '<u>tener</u>' and '<u>poder</u>', you won't go too far wrong. <u>Keep scribbling them down</u> until you know them (or run out of paper).

Irregular Verbs in the Present Tense

And just when you thought things couldn't get any <u>worse</u>, the <u>verbs</u> on this page are all <u>irregular</u>.
I bet page 63 seems like a <u>walk in the park</u> now...

Some of the <u>most useful verbs</u> <u>are</u> irregular

'<u>To be</u>' and '<u>to go</u>' are used <u>all the time</u> so it's worth memorising them <u>now</u>.

To confuse things even more, Spanish has <u>two forms</u> of '<u>to be</u>'.
Learn when to use them on the <u>next page</u>.

ser = to be			
<u>I</u> am =	soy	somos	= <u>we</u> are
<u>you</u> (singular) are =	eres	sois	= <u>you</u> (plural) are
<u>he / she / it</u> is =	es	son	= <u>they</u> are

<u>Don't forget</u> to add the <u>extra accents</u> for '<u>estar</u>'. 'Esta' <u>without</u> the accent means '<u>this</u>'.

estar = to be			
<u>I</u> am =	estoy	estamos	= <u>we</u> are
<u>you</u> (singular) are =	estás	estáis	= <u>you</u> (plural) are
<u>he / she / it</u> is =	está	están	= <u>they</u> are

'<u>To go</u>' is used to make other tenses, e.g. the <u>future tense</u>, so learn it well.

ir = to go			
<u>I</u> go =	voy	vamos	= <u>we</u> go
<u>you</u> (singular) go =	vas	vais	= <u>you</u> (plural) go
<u>he / she / it</u> goes =	va	van	= <u>they</u> go

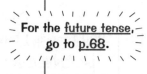

For the <u>future tense</u>, go to <u>p.68</u>.

There is = "hay", it is = "es"

'<u>There is</u>' and '<u>it is</u>' are two quite <u>similar phrases</u> in English. Here's how to say them <u>in Spanish</u>.

1) To say '<u>there is</u>' or '<u>there are</u>' in Spanish, you say '<u>hay</u>' (<u>pronounce</u> it like '<u>eye</u>').

> <u>Hay</u> un armario en mi dormitorio.   <u>There is</u> a wardrobe in my bedroom.

2) To say '<u>it is</u>' in Spanish, use '<u>es</u>' (from the verb '<u>ser</u>').

> Me gusta la película porque <u>es</u> interesante.   I like the film because <u>it's</u> interesting.

Hay a fly in my eye — I'm a poet and I didn't even know it...

<u>Present tense irregular verbs</u> are really annoying, but they're also <u>super important</u>. Just try holding a conversation <u>without</u> any of the verbs from this page. <u>Difficult</u>, eh? Get them learnt, go on.

'Ser' and 'Estar'

Spanish speakers have two verbs that both mean 'to be'. How annoying of them.
You can't just choose 'ser' or 'estar' randomly because they're used in different situations...

Use ser for things that don't change

'Ser' is for talking about permanent things:

Bonjour madame, 'ow are you today?

1) **Nationalities:**

For more nationalities, see p.51.

Soy inglés. I am English.	*Son francesas.* They are French.

2) **Family relationships:**

Ese hombre es mi padre.   That man is my father.

See p.10 for more family relationships and p.22 for more jobs.

3) **Jobs:**

Mi hermano es médico. My brother is a doctor.	*Soy actor.* I am an actor.

4) **Physical characteristics:**

Somos muy altos. We are very tall.	*Su camiseta es verde.* Her T-shirt is green.

For more words for appearance and personality, see p.9.

5) **Personality:**

Eres perezoso. You are lazy.	*Es bastante tímida.* She is quite shy.

Use estar for temporary things and locations

Use 'estar' to talk about something that may change in the future, like a feeling:

Mi amigo está muy contento hoy.   My friend is very happy today.

'Estar' is also used to say where someone or something is:

Estamos en el parque. We are in the park.	*Barcelona está en España.* Barcelona is in Spain.

You ser-iously need to learn this estar-ordinarily helpful page...

Having two ways of saying 'to be' is pretty weird, I'll give you that. But so long as you remember that 'ser' is for permanent things and 'estar' for temporary things and places, you'll be fine.

Reflexive Verbs

Reflexive verbs are actions you do to yourself, like 'washing yourself'.
They're useful if you want to talk about your daily routine in Spanish.

Reflexive verbs have 'se' on the end...

> Grammar Fans: these are 'Reflexive verbs'.

1) Some infinitives have 'se' attached to the end, like 'lavarse'
   or 'despertarse'. These are reflexive verbs.
2) You use a reflexive verb when you want to say that you are doing the action to yourself.
   For example:

   'Lavar' means 'to wash'...   ...but 'lavarse' means 'to get oneself washed'.

   | Lavo el perro. *I wash the dog.* | | Me lavo. *I get washed.* |

   Lots of daily routine verbs
   are reflexive (see p.14).

   See below for forming the reflexive.

Here are some examples
of reflexive verbs:

to wake up:	despertarse	to get washed:	lavarse
to get up:	levantarse	to get dressed:	vestirse
to get showered:	ducharse	to go to bed:	acostarse

People doing stuff — me levanto, me lavo...

The 'se' bit on reflexive verbs means oneself. This bit changes depending on who is
doing the action. All the different ways of saying 'se' ('oneself') are in blue:

The endings are the same as regular verbs (see p.62).

lavarse = to get washed			
I get washed =	me lavo	nos lavamos	= we get washed
you (singular) get washed =	te lavas	os laváis	= you (plural) get washed
he / she / it gets washed =	se lava	se lavan	= they get washed

This lot literally means 'I wash myself', 'you wash yourself', etc.

Here's how to form reflexive verbs. This example is for 'I get up':

1. Move 'se' in front of the verb and change it to the right part.

   | levantarse | ➜ | se + levantar | ➜ | me + levantar |

2. Change the ending of 'levantar' to match the person.

   | me + levantar | ➜ | me + levanto | | me levanto = I get up. |

I wash myself — well done, now dress yourself...

Reflexive verbs can seem pretty daunting, but if you split them up into the 'self word' and the verb,
it's doable. Write out your daily routine until you can do it without peeking back at this page.

Making Sentences Negative

This is a pessimist's <u>dream page</u>. Even if you've got a more <u>positive outlook</u> on life, it's <u>important</u> to get to grips with how to form <u>negative sentences</u>.

Use 'no' to say <u>not</u>

1) In Spanish, if you want a verb to have the <u>opposite meaning</u>, you put '<u>no</u>' <u>in front</u> of the <u>verb</u>.

Me llamo Salvador.
= I am called Salvador.

<u>No</u> me llamo Salvador.*
= I am <u>not</u> called Salvador.

*Me llamo Pablo Picasso.

'<u>Me llamo</u>' is the verb.
The '<u>no</u>' goes <u>in front</u>.

2) You do the <u>same</u> with <u>all verbs</u>:

<u>No</u> puedo venir.
= I can't come.

'puedo venir' and 'juego' are the verbs. The '<u>no</u>' goes <u>in front</u>.

<u>No</u> juego al fútbol.
= I don't play football.

Never = 'nunca', nothing = 'nada'

There are two <u>other</u> negative phrases you need to learn...

1) To say '<u>nothing</u>': no + verb nada

Aquí no hay nada.
There's <u>nothing</u> here.

No hace nada.
He does <u>nothing</u>.

THE GOLDEN RULE
Put the 'no' before the verb and the 'nada' or 'nunca' after the verb.

2) To say '<u>never</u>': no + verb nunca

No voy nunca a la piscina.
I <u>never</u> go to the swimming pool.

No ayuda nunca.
She <u>never</u> helps.

It would also be <u>correct</u> to say "<u>nunca voy a la piscina</u>" or "<u>nunca ayuda</u>". See <u>p.73</u> for more.

Spot the sombrero...

Put a <u>cross</u> where you think the <u>sombrero</u> might be. You can have up to <u>five</u> crosses. <u>Ten bonus points</u> if you know their <u>names</u>...

Talking about the Future

Teachers love asking you about <u>the future</u> — what you're <u>going to be</u> when you're older, where you're <u>going to go</u> on holiday, etc. Here's how to tackle their <u>interrogations</u>...

What is the future tense?

1) You use the <u>future tense</u> to talk about events that are <u>going to happen</u> in the <u>future</u>.

2) There are <u>two ways</u> to talk about the future in Spanish. <u>This one</u>, you'll be pleased to know, is the <u>easy way</u>. You can look forward to a different way at GCSE.

You can use 'I'm going to' to talk about the future

To form the <u>future tense</u>, there are <u>three easy parts</u>:

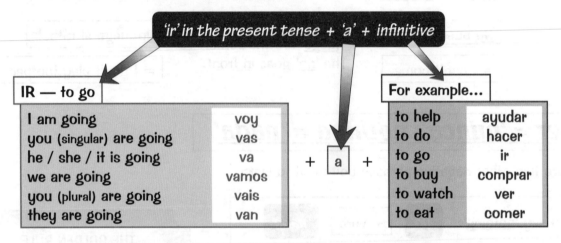

> 'ir' in the present tense + 'a' + infinitive

IR — to go

I am going	voy
you (singular) are going	vas
he / she / it is going	va
we are going	vamos
you (plural) are going	vais
they are going	van

+ a +

For example...

to help	ayudar
to do	hacer
to go	ir
to buy	comprar
to watch	ver
to eat	comer

EXAMPLES

¿Vas a ir al cine hoy? *Are you going to go to the cinema today?*

Voy a hacer mis deberes. *I am going to do my homework.*

Van a jugar al tenis. *They are going to play tennis.*

Juan va a comprar un jersey. *Juan is going to buy a jumper.*

Let's go back to the future...

You're in luck here only having to learn the <u>easy future tense</u>. But d'you know what that means? You've got to memorise it until you can <u>talk about your future perfectly</u>, standing on your head.

Giving Orders

Just imagine if you could be <u>bossy in Spanish</u>... Fun, eh? Having said that, you're <u>more likely</u> to <u>hear</u> your <u>teacher</u> bossing you around, so make sure you <u>understand</u> all of these commands.

You need this stuff for giving informal orders

To give orders in Spanish, just <u>take the 's'</u> off the '<u>you (singular)</u>' part of the verb. These are <u>informal commands</u> for <u>one person</u>, so they're just for people you <u>know well</u>, like <u>family</u> and <u>friends</u>.

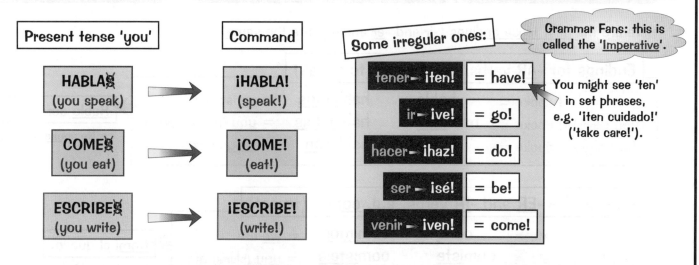

Present tense 'you'		Command
HABLAS̶ (you speak)	→	¡HABLA! (speak!)
COMES̶ (you eat)	→	¡COME! (eat!)
ESCRIBES̶ (you write)	→	¡ESCRIBE! (write!)

Some irregular ones:

tener→ ¡ten!	= have!
ir→ ¡ve!	= go!
hacer→ ¡haz!	= do!
ser → ¡sé!	= be!
venir→ ¡ven!	= come!

Grammar Fans: this is called the '<u>Imperative</u>'.

You might see 'ten' in set phrases, e.g. 'ten cuidado!' ('take care!').

And for politely telling someone what to do

Telling someone what to do <u>politely</u> is a bit <u>trickier</u>. You need to <u>memorise</u> these <u>endings</u>:

-AR verbs

For -<u>ar</u> verbs, take the '<u>he/she/it</u>' form of the <u>present tense</u> and then <u>swap</u> the final '<u>a</u>' for an '<u>e</u>'.

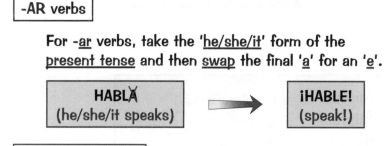

HABLA̶ (he/she/it speaks)	→	¡HABLE! (speak!)

Luckily for you, for telling more than one person what to do, you'll have to wait until GCSE. Hurray!

-ER and -IR verbs

For -<u>er</u> and -<u>ir</u> verbs, take the '<u>he/she/it</u>' form of the <u>present tense</u> and then <u>swap</u> the final '<u>e</u>' for an '<u>a</u>'.

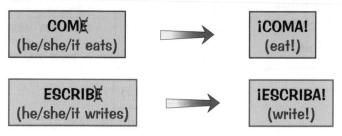

COME̶ (he/she/it eats)	→	¡COMA! (eat!)
ESCRIBE̶ (he/she/it writes)	→	¡ESCRIBA! (write!)

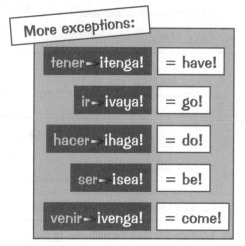

More exceptions:

tener→ ¡tenga!	= have!
ir→ ¡vaya!	= go!
hacer→ ¡haga!	= do!
ser→ ¡sea!	= be!
venir→ ¡venga!	= come!

Repeat after me — learn this page, learn this page...

Unfortunately for you, there's <u>more chance</u> you'll be bossed around by your teacher than give out any orders. But learn this page so you <u>understand what they're telling you to do</u> in Spanish classes.

Talking about the Past

Knowing how to <u>talk about the past</u> is just as important as being able to talk about the future...

Use the past tense to talk about the past

Grammar Fans: this is called the 'Preterite Tense'.

This is <u>how to form</u> the <u>past tense</u> in Spanish:

1 Find the verb stem by removing the last two letters of the infinitive.   **2** Add on the new ending.

Here are the <u>past tense endings</u> (-<u>ir</u> and -<u>er</u> endings are the <u>same</u>):

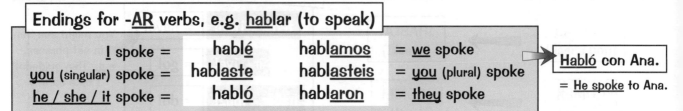

Endings for -**AR** verbs, e.g. <u>hablar</u> (to speak)		
<u>I</u> spoke =	hab<u>lé</u> hab<u>lamos</u>	= <u>we</u> spoke
<u>you</u> (singular) spoke =	hab<u>laste</u> hab<u>lasteis</u>	= <u>you</u> (plural) spoke
<u>he / she / it</u> spoke =	hab<u>ló</u> hab<u>laron</u>	= <u>they</u> spoke

<u>Habló</u> con Ana.

= <u>He spoke</u> to Ana.

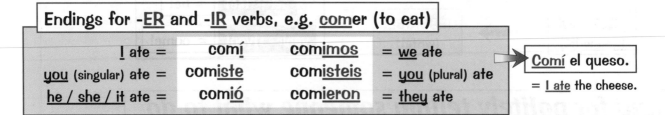

Endings for -**ER** and -**IR** verbs, e.g. <u>comer</u> (to eat)		
<u>I</u> ate =	com<u>í</u> com<u>imos</u>	= <u>we</u> ate
<u>you</u> (singular) ate =	com<u>iste</u> com<u>isteis</u>	= <u>you</u> (plural) ate
<u>he / she / it</u> ate =	com<u>ió</u> com<u>ieron</u>	= <u>they</u> ate

<u>Comí</u> el queso.

= <u>I ate</u> the cheese.

Some important irregular verbs in the past

More <u>really useful irregular verbs</u> for you. Have fun...

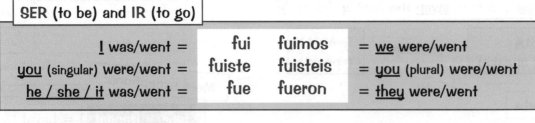

SER (to be) and IR (to go)		
<u>I</u> was/went =	fui fuimos	= <u>we</u> were/went
<u>you</u> (singular) were/went =	fuiste fuisteis	= <u>you</u> (plural) were/went
<u>he / she / it</u> was/went =	fue fueron	= <u>they</u> were/went

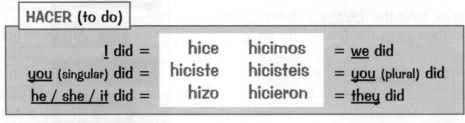

HACER (to do)		
<u>I</u> did =	hice hicimos	= <u>we</u> did
<u>you</u> (singular) did =	hiciste hicisteis	= <u>you</u> (plural) did
<u>he / she / it</u> did =	hizo hicieron	= <u>they</u> did

And don't forget — use the '<u>he/she/it</u>' part to form <u>polite 'you</u>' (<u>singular</u>) and the '<u>they</u>' part for the <u>polite 'you</u>' (<u>plural</u>).

<u>Fui</u> a la playa — <u>fue</u> excelente.

= <u>I went</u> to the beach — <u>it was</u> excellent.

¿Qué <u>hiciste</u> ayer?

= What <u>did you do</u> yesterday?

Dinosaurs and teachers — they both love the past...
Okay, so you're not wrinkly and grey enough to be whipping out the 'when I was a kid' line, but being able to <u>say what you did yesterday</u> is dead useful. Get all the <u>endings</u> learnt <u>off by heart</u>.

Useful Small Words

It's always the <u>little ones</u> which cause problems... Here are the <u>most important</u> small words.

Talking is tricky without 'to', 'at', 'from' and 'of'...

To = a

'<u>a</u>' + '<u>el</u>' = '<u>al</u>'

'<u>To</u>' is usually '<u>a</u>':

*Voy **a** casa.*   I'm going (<u>to</u>) home.

*Va **a** Bilbao.*   He's going <u>to</u> Bilbao.

At = en, a

'<u>At</u>' is also sometimes '<u>a</u>'...

A las cinco.   <u>At</u> five o'clock.

...but sometimes '<u>en</u>' means '<u>at</u>' too.

En casa.   <u>At</u> home.

From = de

'<u>de</u>' + '<u>el</u>' = '<u>del</u>'

'<u>From</u>' is usually written as '<u>de</u>':

*Soy **de** Cumbria.*   I'm <u>from</u> Cumbria.

*Es **del** aula.*   It's <u>from the</u> classroom.

Of = de

When we say '<u>of</u>', Spanish people say '<u>de</u>':

*Una botella **de** zumo.* A bottle <u>of</u> juice.

*Un bocadillo **de** jamón.*   A ham sandwich.

(Literally a 'sandwich <u>of</u> ham')

Learn these words for saying where something is

Knowing how to say <u>where things are</u> is dead <u>useful</u>. These mice will <u>help you out</u>.

Grammar Fans: these are '<u>Prepositions</u>'.

IN
El ratón está <u>en</u> el zapato.
The mouse is <u>in</u> the shoe.

ON
El ratón está <u>sobre</u> la mesa.
The mouse is <u>on</u> the table.
You can also use '<u>en</u>' for '<u>on</u>' too.

NEXT TO
El ratón está <u>al lado de</u> la mesa.
The mouse is <u>next to</u> the table.

BEHIND
El ratón está <u>detrás de</u> la mesa.
The mouse is <u>behind</u> the table.

IN FRONT OF
El ratón está <u>delante de</u> la mesa.
The mouse is <u>in front of</u> the table.

UNDER
El ratón está <u>debajo de</u> la mesa.
The mouse is <u>under</u> the table.

Preposition — 'pre' in front of 'position'...

I always find the small words <u>difficult</u> to remember too, but the more you <u>practise</u>, the <u>easier</u> it'll be.

Small Linking Words

Learn these little <u>linking words</u> to help you <u>join sentences together</u>. They're really <u>useful</u> and they work like the <u>English linking words</u> so it's E.A.S.Y.

> Grammar Fans: these are called the '<u>Conjunctions</u>' or '<u>Connectives</u>'.

Y = And

| Desayuna cereales.
She has cereal for breakfast. | **AND** | Desayuna fruta.
She has fruit for breakfast. | **=** | Desayuna cereales y fruta.
She has cereal <u>and</u> fruit for breakfast. |

The only <u>exception</u> is when '<u>y</u>' comes <u>before</u> a <u>word beginning</u> with '<u>i</u>' or '<u>hi</u>'. If this happens, change the '<u>y</u>' to an '<u>e</u>': 'Estudio español <u>e</u> inglés.' = 'I study Spanish <u>and</u> English.'

O = Or

| Como pasta
a la una.
I eat pasta at 1 o'clock. | **OR** | Como una pizza
a la una.
I eat a pizza at 1 o'clock. | **=** | Como pasta o una pizza a la una.
I eat pasta <u>or</u> a pizza at 1 o'clock. |

When '<u>o</u>' comes <u>before</u> a <u>word beginning</u> with '<u>o</u>' or '<u>ho</u>', it changes to '<u>u</u>': '¿Hay siete <u>u</u> ocho alumnos?' = 'Are there seven <u>or</u> eight pupils?'

Pero = But

> Don't get 'pero' confused with 'perro' ('dog').

| Me gustan
las fresas.
I like strawberries. | **BUT** | No me gustan
las manzanas.
I don't like apples. | **=** | Me gustan las fresas pero
no me gustan las manzanas.
I like strawberries <u>but</u> I don't like apples. |

Porque = Because

Eeh Pam, have you seen our Jeff lately?

Oh yeah, he's looking a bit 'porque' isn't he

'<u>Porque</u>' is really important for being able to <u>explain yourself</u> and <u>give a reason</u>.

| Me gusta esquiar.
I like skiing. | **BECAUSE** | Es divertido.
It's fun. | **=** | Me gusta esquiar porque es divertido.
I like skiing <u>because</u> it's fun. |

Good things come in small packages...

These little <u>joining words</u> will <u>improve</u> your writing no end. Try to write out as many sentences as possible using <u>at least</u> one joining word. I bet you can't make a sentence with <u>three</u> of these in it...

Section 8 — Grammar and Phrases

How Often and How Much

Teachers love <u>detail</u>. Saying you go swimming <u>twice a week</u> is better than boring old "I go swimming". Saying you're <u>very</u> happy is <u>much more exciting</u> than "I'm happy" too.

Say <u>how often</u> <u>you do things</u>

> Grammar Fans: these are called '<u>Adverbs</u>'.

The words you use to say <u>how often you do things</u> are called '<u>adverbs</u>'.
Here are <u>four adverbs</u> to get you started. Use these to say <u>how often</u> (or <u>rarely</u>) you do things:

These two adverbs can go <u>before</u> the <u>verb</u>. Or, they can <u>also</u> go <u>after</u> the <u>verb</u> if you put '<u>no</u>' before the <u>verb</u>. See <u>p.67</u> for more ways to use '<u>nunca</u>'.

nunca = *never*

apenas = *rarely*

a menudo = *often*

siempre = *always*

Anabel apenas juega al tenis.
Anabel <u>rarely</u> plays tennis.

A menudo veo la televisión.
I <u>often</u> watch television.

And the good news is that <u>these adverbs don't change</u>. Hooray!

Helena siempre escucha la radio.
Helena <u>always</u> listens to the radio.

Los chicos siempre escuchan la radio.
The boys <u>always</u> listen to the radio.

Use these <u>three words</u> <u>to give</u> even more detail

Use these words to say <u>how much</u> something is done.
For example, instead of saying rugby is "<u>good</u>", say rugby is "<u>quite good</u>", or "<u>very good</u>".

muy = *very*

bastante = *quite*

<u>'Too much'</u> here <u>describes</u> the <u>verb</u>. If you use 'too much' <u>to describe a noun</u>, e.g. 'too much lettuce' ('demasiad<u>a</u> lechuga'), 'demasiado' <u>agrees</u>.

Estoy muy cansado.
I'm <u>very</u> tired.

'<u>Very</u>' <u>describes</u> the <u>adjective</u> ('tired').

demasiado = *too much*

Hablas demasiado.
You talk <u>too much</u>.

I'm very tired — I study too much...

There are a <u>few adverbs to learn</u> on this page, but they're useful for <u>adding extra information</u> to your sentences. And if you <u>willingly give more details</u>, your teacher will ask <u>fewer questions</u>. Win.

Summary Questions

There's loads of grammar in this section and it's mega-important that you know it, so take your time and answer all of the questions. Then you'll deserve a chocolatey treat. Or maybe you'd prefer something more Spanishy, like a paella, now that you're a Spanish expert...

1) How would you say these in Spanish? a) I love to swim because it's fun.
b) I hate French because it's difficult.

2) Write a question in Spanish using each of these question words:
a) ¿qué?   b) ¿cómo?   c) ¿dónde?   d) ¿cuánto?

3) Turn these Spanish words into plurals: a) la camisa   b) el brazo c) el lápiz

4) Copy and complete these tables for 'the', 'a' and 'some':

THE	MASCULINE	FEMININE
SINGULAR		
PLURAL		

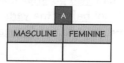

A	
MASCULINE	FEMININE

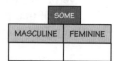

SOME	
MASCULINE	FEMININE

5) Rewrite each sentence, replacing the underlined nouns with the correct pronoun:
a) <u>Tomás y Pedro</u> limpian <u>la casa</u>.   b) <u>Vanessa y Helen</u> compran <u>las galletas</u>.

6) Reinaldo wants a new hat. How would he say this in Spanish?

7) Reinaldo reckons his new hat is the best. How would he say this in Spanish?

8) In Spanish, how would Reinaldo say "That hat is my hat."

9) That's enough about Reinaldo's hat. What do these sentences mean in English?
a) Fui por el mercado por la mañana. b) Quiero ir a Cumbria para hacer ciclismo para un mes.

10) 'Ayudar' (to help) is a regular -ar verb. How would you say: a) I help b) he helps c) we help

11) What do these mean in English? a) quiero b) podemos c) tienes d) pueden e) queréis

12) Write these in English: a) vas b) voy c) vais d) van e) va f) vamos

13) a) 'Ser' means 'to be'. Say these using 'ser': a) I am b) you (plural) are c) he is d) they are
b) 'Estar' also means 'to be'. Using 'estar', what is: a) I am b) she is c) we are d) they are

14) How would you say "there is a mouse in my shoe" in Spanish? Now say "it's big".

15) Write these in Spanish: a) I'm Scottish b) He's kind c) They're sad today d) We're in Madrid

16) Use 'ducharse' to write: a) I get showered b) he gets showered c) we get showered

17) Write these in Spanish: a) He can't come b) I never eat rice c) They do nothing on Sundays

18) What are these in English: a) Voy a ir al parque b) Van a cenar c) Vamos a ayudar a mi tío

19) Your teacher says, "¡Escribe tu nombre!". What is he/she telling you to do?

20) How do you say: a) I went to the cinema — it was boring b) They did their homework

21) What's the Spanish for: a) I'm going to Wales b) He's from Cheshire c) A cheese sandwich

22) What do these mean: a) el gato está sobre la mesa b) el perro está delante del sofá

23) In Spanish, write: a) I like geography and German b) I listen to the radio or watch television

24) What do these mean: a) Nunca voy al cine b) Siempre escucha música c) Comen demasiado

Index

Index

Ahoy there! That's it for KS3 Spanish. Farewell, landlubbers...